everyday

chicken

This is a Parragon book
First published in 2007

Parragon
Queen Street House
4 Queen Street
Bath BA1 1HE, UK

Copyright © Parragon Books Ltd 2007
Designed by Terry Jeavons & Company

ISBN 978-1-4054-9394-9

Printed in China

This book uses imperial and metric measurements. Follow the same units of measurement throughout; do not mix imperial and metric. All spoon measurements are level, unless otherwise stated: teaspoons are assumed to be 5ml and tablespoons are assumed to be 15ml. Unless otherwise stated, milk is assumed to be whole, eggs and individual fruits such as bananas are medium and pepper is freshly ground black pepper.

Recipes using raw or very lightly cooked eggs should be avoided by infants, the elderly, pregnant women, convalescents and anyone suffering from an illness. Pregnant and breast-feeding women are advised to avoid eating peanuts and peanut products.

everyday
chicken

introduction

Chicken has become one of the most useful and popular meats in nearly all cultures around the world. The reasons for this are many, not least that chickens are relatively quick and easy to raise, and do not require acres of lush grassland! It is worth bearing in mind that a free-range, corn-fed chicken might cost a little more, but it will have a far superior flavour to one that has been intensively farmed.

From a nutritional point of view, chicken is an excellent source of protein, B vitamins and minerals such as zinc and iron. It is naturally low in fat and has no carbohydrates, making it the dream

food for those who need to keep their weight or cholesterol levels in check. It is very quick and easy to cook, too, so there need be no excuses about not having enough time to produce a healthy, well-balanced meal!

And from a gastronomic point of view? There are so many options that you could serve chicken every day of the week and still not run out of ideas! Chicken can be cooked very simply – roasted, chargrilled, grilled, stir-fried

or pan-fried – and served with potatoes or rice and salad leaves or lightly cooked vegetables. And when you have a little more time to spare, the choices are endless. If you like rice, you can go for a creamy Italian risotto or a saffron-coloured Spanish paella; and if you are a pasta lover, you will find some fantastic sauces and might even be inspired to make your own filled pasta shapes, such as tortellini and ravioli. If Mexican food is your thing, there are recipes for fajitas, tacos and tostadas; and there are Chinese, Thai and

Indian dishes to satisfy spice cravings!

Some recipes are specifically for those who are diabetic, or follow a low-fat, low-carb or gluten-free diet – check in the introduction to each chapter for ideas. And whatever your reason for choosing chicken – good health!

soups, starters & salads

Chicken and soup seem made for each other, and this chapter has a handful of chicken soups, each with a completely different character, from a light and delicious Clear Soup with Mushrooms & Chicken to a creamy and elegant Chicken & Tarragon Soup. Chicken, Avocado & Chipotle Soup is a Mexican recipe with attitude, and if you are feeling blue, treat yourself to a bowl of Chicken-Noodle Soup, the classic cure-all!

Chicken is a useful ingredient in appetizers. Spanish tapas bars serve it in the form of Crispy Chicken & Ham Croquettes and Chicken in Lemon & Garlic, while smooth, rich Chicken Liver Pâté is a speciality of French bistros. Tantalizingly aromatic Soy Chicken Wings are a typical Chinese snack, irresistibly messy to eat.

A chicken salad can be as simple as you like, but it need not be dull. Chicken and blue cheese are natural partners, as you will discover if you try Chicken, Cheese & Rocket Salad or Chicken Pinwheels with Blue Cheese & Herbs. Chicken loves spices, too – Cajun Chicken Salad and Red Chicken Salad are great examples of this. And if you want a chicken salad that is very low in fat but big on style, try the Thai Chicken Salad – it looks and tastes so good, you certainly won't feel deprived!

chicken & broccoli soup

ingredients

SERVES 4–6

225 g/8 oz head broccoli
salt and pepper
55 g/2 oz unsalted butter
1 onion, chopped
225 g/8 oz basmati rice
225 g/8 oz skinless, boneless
   chicken breast, cut into
   thin slivers
25 g/1 oz plain wholewheat
   flour
300 ml/10 fl oz milk
500 ml/16 fl oz chicken stock
55 g/2 oz sweetcorn kernels

method

1 Break the broccoli into small florets and cook in a saucepan of lightly salted boiling water for 3 minutes, drain, then plunge into cold water and set aside.

2 Melt the butter in a pan over medium heat, add the onion, rice and chicken, and cook for 5 minutes, stirring frequently.

3 Remove the pan from the heat and stir in the flour. Return to the heat and cook for 2 minutes, stirring constantly. Stir in the milk and then the stock. Bring to the boil, stirring constantly, then reduce the heat and simmer for 10 minutes.

4 Drain the broccoli and add to the pan with the sweetcorn, salt and pepper. Simmer for a further 5 minutes, or until the rice is tender, then serve.

chicken & tarragon soup

ingredients

SERVES 4

55 g/2 oz unsalted butter
1 large onion, chopped
300 g/10$^{1}/_{2}$ oz cooked
   skinless chicken,
   shredded finely
625 ml/20 fl oz chicken stock
salt and pepper
1 tbsp chopped fresh tarragon
150 ml/5 fl oz double cream
fresh tarragon leaves, to garnish
deep-fried crôutons, to serve

method

1 Melt the butter in a large saucepan and fry the onion for 3 minutes.

2 Add the chicken to the pan with half of the chicken stock. Bring to the boil, then reduce the heat and simmer for 20 minutes. Let cool, then process until smooth in a blender or food processor.

3 Add the remainder of the stock and season with salt and pepper.

4 Add the chopped tarragon, then transfer the soup to individual serving bowls and stir in the cream.

5 Garnish the soup with fresh tarragon and serve with deep-fried crôutons.

chicken, avocado & chipotle soup

ingredients

SERVES 4

1.6 litres/50 fl oz chicken
    stock

2–3 garlic cloves, finely
    chopped

1–2 dried chipotle chillies, cut
    into very thin strips

1 avocado

lime or lemon juice, for tossing

3–5 spring onions, thinly
    sliced

350–400 g/12–14 oz cooked
    chicken breast meat, torn or
    cut into shreds or thin strips

2 tbsp chopped fresh
    coriander

1 lime, cut into wedges, and
    handful of tortilla chips
    (optional), to serve

method

1 Place the stock in a large, heavy-based saucepan with the garlic and chillies and bring to the boil.

2 Meanwhile, cut the avocado in half around the stone. Twist apart, then remove the stone with a knife. Carefully peel off the skin, dice the flesh and immediately toss in lime juice to prevent discoloration.

3 Arrange the spring onions, chicken, avocado and coriander in the bottom of 4 soup bowls or in a large serving bowl.

4 Ladle the hot stock over and serve with lime wedges and a handful of tortilla chips, if wished.

clear soup with mushrooms & chicken

ingredients

SERVES 4

25 g/1 oz dried cèpes or other
    mushrooms
1 litre/32 fl oz water
2 tbsp vegetable or peanut oil
115 g/4 oz mushrooms,
    sliced
2 garlic cloves, chopped
    coarsely
5-cm/2-inch piece fresh
    galangal, sliced thinly
2 chicken breast portions
    (on the bone, skin on)
225 g/8 oz baby chestnut or
    white mushrooms, cut into
    quarters
juice of 1/2 lime
sprigs fresh flat-leaf parsley,
    to garnish

method

1 Place the dried mushrooms in a small bowl and pour over hot water to cover. Set aside to soak for 20–30 minutes. Drain the mushrooms, reserving the soaking liquid. Cut off and discard the stalks and chop the caps coarsely.

2 Pour the reserved soaking water into a saucepan with the measured water and bring to the boil. Reduce the heat to a simmer.

3 Meanwhile, heat the oil in a wok and stir-fry the soaked mushrooms, sliced fresh mushrooms, garlic and galangal for 3–4 minutes. Add to the pan of hot water with the chicken breasts. Simmer for 10–15 minutes, until the meat comes off the bones easily.

4 Remove the chicken from the pan. Peel off and set aside the skin. Remove the meat from the bones, slice and set aside. Return the skin and bones to the stock and simmer for a further 30 minutes.

5 Remove the pan from the heat and strain the stock into a clean pan through a sieve lined with cheesecloth. Bring back to the boil and add the chestnut or white mushrooms, sliced chicken and lime juice. Reduce the heat and simmer for 8-10 minutes. Ladle into warmed bowls, garnish with parsley sprigs and serve immediately.

thai chicken-coconut soup

ingredients

SERVES 4

115 g/4 oz dried
    cellophane noodles
1.25 litres/40 fl oz chicken or
    vegetable stock
1 lemon grass stalk, crushed
1-cm/$^1/_2$-inch piece fresh root
    ginger, peeled and very
    finely chopped
2 fresh kaffir lime leaves,
    thinly sliced
1 fresh red chilli, or to taste,
    deseeded and thinly sliced
2 skinless, boneless chicken
    breasts, thinly sliced
225 g/8 oz coconut cream
2 tbsp nam pla (Thai fish sauce)
about 1 tbsp fresh lime juice
55 g/2 oz beansprouts
green part of 4 spring onions,
    finely sliced
fresh coriander leaves,
    to garnish

method

1 Soak the dried noodles in a large bowl with enough lukewarm water to cover for 20 minutes, until soft. Alternatively, cook according to the packet instructions. Drain well and set aside.

2 Meanwhile, bring the stock to the boil in a large saucepan over high heat. Lower the heat, add the lemon grass, ginger, lime leaves and chilli and simmer for 5 minutes. Add the chicken and continue simmering for a further 3 minutes, or until the flesh is poached. Stir in the coconut cream, nam pla and most of the lime juice and continue simmering for 3 minutes. Add the beansprouts and spring onions and simmer for a further 1 minute. Taste and gradually add extra nam pla or lime juice at this point, if you like. Remove and discard the lemongrass stalk.

3 Divide the noodles between 4 bowls. Bring the soup back to the boil, then add the soup to each bowl. The heat of the soup will warm the noodles. Serve garnished with coriander leaves.

chicken-noodle soup

ingredients

SERVES 4–6

2 skinless chicken breasts

2 litres/64 fl oz water

1 onion, with skin left on,
    cut in half

1 large garlic clove, cut in half

1-cm/^{1}/$_2$-inch piece fresh root
    ginger, peeled and sliced

4 black peppercorns, lightly
    crushed

4 cloves

2 star anise

salt and pepper

1 carrot, peeled

1 celery stalk, chopped

100 g/3^1/$_2$ oz baby corn, cut
    in half lengthways and
    chopped

2 spring onions, finely
    shredded

115 g/4 oz dried rice
    vermicelli noodles

method

1 Put the chicken breasts and water in a saucepan over high heat and bring to the boil. Lower the heat to its lowest setting and simmer, skimming the surface until no more foam rises. Add the onion, garlic, ginger, peppercorns, cloves, star anise and a pinch of salt and continue to simmer for 20 minutes, or until the chicken is tender and cooked through. Meanwhile, grate the carrot along its length on the coarse side of a grater so you get long, thin strips.

2 Strain the chicken, reserving about 1.25 litres/40 fl oz stock, but discarding any flavouring ingredients. (At this point you can let the stock cool and refrigerate overnight, so any fat solidifies and can be lifted off and discarded.) Return the stock to the rinsed-out pan with the carrot, celery, baby corn and spring onions and bring to the boil. Boil until the baby corn are almost tender, then add the noodles and continue boiling for 2 minutes.

3 Meanwhile, chop the chicken, add it to the pan and continue cooking for about 1 minute until the chicken is reheated and the noodles are soft. Add seasoning.

whole chicken soup

ingredients

SERVES 6–8

100 g/3¹/₂ oz Yunnan ham or
    ordinary ham, chopped

2 dried Chinese mushrooms,
    soaked in warm water for
    20 minutes

85 g/3 oz fresh or canned
    bamboo shoots, rinsed (if
    using fresh shoots, boil in
    water first for 30 minutes)

1 whole chicken

1 tbsp slivered spring onion

8 slices fresh root ginger

225 g/8 oz lean pork, chopped

2 tsp Shaoxing rice wine

2.8 litres/96 fl oz water

2 tsp salt

300 g/10¹/₂ oz Chinese
    cabbage, cut into
    large chunks

sesame & spring onion dipping sauce

2 tbsp light soy sauce

¹/₄ tsp sesame oil

2 tsp finely chopped spring
    onion

method

1 To make the dipping sauce, combine all the ingredients in a small bowl and set aside.

2 Blanch the Yunnan ham in boiling water for 30 seconds. Skim the surface, then remove the ham and set aside. Squeeze out any excess water from the mushrooms, then finely slice, discarding any tough stems. Chop the bamboo shoots into small cubes.

3 Stuff the chicken with the spring onion and ginger. Put all the ingredients, except the cabbage and dipping sauce, in a casserole. Bring to the boil, then lower the heat and simmer, covered, for 1 hour. Add the cabbage and simmer for a further 3 minutes.

4 Remove the chicken skin before serving, then place a chunk of chicken meat in each individual bowl, adding pieces of vegetable and the other meats, and pour the soup on top. Serve with the dipping sauce.

chicken crostini

ingredients

SERVES 4

12 slices French bread or
    country bread

4 tbsp olive oil

2 garlic cloves, chopped

2 tbsp finely chopped fresh
    oregano

salt and pepper

100 g/3^1/$_2$ oz cold roast
    chicken, cut into small,
    thin slices

4 tomatoes, sliced

12 thin slices of goat's cheese

12 black olives, pitted
    and chopped

fresh red and green salad
    leaves, to serve

method

1 Put the bread under a preheated medium grill and lightly toast on both sides. Meanwhile, pour the olive oil into a bowl and add the garlic and oregano. Season with salt and pepper and mix well. Remove the toasted bread slices from the grill and brush them on one side only with the oil mixture.

2 Place the bread slices, oiled sides up, on a baking sheet. Put some sliced chicken on top of each one, followed by a slice of tomato.

3 Divide the slices of goat's cheese among the bread slices, then top with the chopped olives. Drizzle over the remaining oil mixture and transfer to a preheated oven, 180°C/ 350°F/Gas Mark 4. Bake for about 5 minutes, or until the cheese is golden brown and starting to melt.

4 Remove from the oven and serve with fresh red and green salad leaves.

crispy chicken & ham croquettes

ingredients

MAKES 8

4 tbsp olive oil

4 tbsp plain flour

200 ml/7 fl oz milk

115 g/4 oz cooked chicken, ground

55 g/2 oz serrano or cooked ham, very finely chopped

1 tbsp chopped fresh flat-leaf parsley, plus extra sprigs to garnish

small pinch of freshly grated nutmeg

salt and pepper

1 egg, beaten

55 g/2 oz day-old white breadcrumbs

corn oil, for deep-frying

garlic mayonnaise, to serve

method

1 Heat the olive oil in a saucepan. Stir in the flour to form a paste and cook gently for 1 minute, stirring constantly. Gradually stir in the milk until smooth and slowly bring to the boil, stirring constantly, until the mixture boils and thickens.

2 Remove from the heat, add the ground chicken and beat until the mixture is smooth. Add the chopped ham, parsley and nutmeg and mix well together. Season with salt and pepper. Put in a dish and let stand for 30 minutes, until cool, then cover and let rest in the refrigerator for 2–3 hours or overnight.

3 Pour the beaten egg onto a plate and spread out the breadcrumbs on another plate. Divide the chilled chicken mixture into 8 portions, then shape to form cylindrical croquettes. Dip them, one at a time, in the beaten egg, then roll in the breadcrumbs to coat. Let chill in the refrigerator for 1 hour.

4 Heat the oil in a deep-fryer to 180–190ºC/ 350–375ºF. Add the croquettes, in batches to prevent the temperature of the oil dropping, and deep-fry for 5–10 minutes, or until golden brown and crispy. Remove with a slotted spoon and drain well on kitchen paper.

5 Serve the croquettes piping hot, garnished with parsley sprigs, with garlic mayonnaise.

chicken liver pâté

ingredients

MAKES 8–10 SLICES

175 g/6 oz unsalted butter
500 g/1 lb 2 oz chicken livers,
    thawed if frozen,
    and trimmed
$1/2$ tbsp sunflower oil
2 shallots, finely chopped
2 large garlic cloves, finely
    chopped
$2^1/2$ tbsp Madeira or brandy
2 tbsp double cream
1 tsp dried thyme
$1/4$ tsp ground allspice
salt and pepper
toasted slices brioche and
    mixed salad leaves,
    to serve

method

1 Melt 25 g/1 oz of the butter in a large frying pan over medium–high heat. Add the chicken livers and stir for 5 minutes, or until they are brown on the outside, but still slightly pink in the centres. Work in batches, if necessary, to avoid overcrowding the pan.

2 Transfer the livers and their cooking juices to a food processor. Melt another 25 g/1 oz of the butter with the oil in the pan. Add the shallots and garlic and sauté, stirring frequently, for 2–3 minutes, until the shallots are soft, but not brown.

3 Add the Madeira and scrape up any cooking juices from the base. Stir in the cream, then the thyme, allspice, salt and pepper. Pour this mixture, with the cooking juices, into the food processor with the livers. Add the remaining butter, cut into small pieces.

4 Whiz the mixture in the food processor until smooth. Taste, and adjust the seasoning if necessary. Let the mixture cool slightly, then scrape into a serving bowl and set aside to allow the pâté to cool completely.

5 Serve immediately, or cover and store in the refrigerator for up to 3 days and let stand at room temperature for 30 minutes before serving. Serve with hot toasted brioche and mixed salad leaves.

chicken in lemon & garlic

ingredients

SERVES 6–8

4 large skinless, boneless
    chicken breasts

5 tbsp Spanish olive oil

1 onion, finely chopped

6 garlic cloves,
    finely chopped

grated rind of 1 lemon, finely
    pared rind of 1 lemon and
    juice of both lemons

4 tbsp chopped fresh
    flat-leaf parsley, plus extra
    to garnish

salt and pepper

lemon wedges and crusty
    bread (optional), to serve

method

1 Using a sharp knife, slice the chicken breasts widthways into very thin slices. Heat the olive oil in a large, heavy-based frying pan, add the onion and cook for 5 minutes, or until softened, but not browned. Add the garlic and cook for a further 30 seconds.

2 Add the sliced chicken to the pan and cook gently for 5–10 minutes, stirring from time to time, until all the ingredients are lightly browned and the chicken is tender.

3 Add the grated lemon rind and the lemon juice and let it bubble. At the same time, deglaze the pan by scraping and stirring all the bits on the bottom of the pan into the juices with a wooden spoon. Remove the skillet from the heat, stir in the parsley and season with salt and pepper.

4 Transfer, piping hot, to a warmed serving dish. Sprinkle with the pared lemon rind, garnish with the parsley and serve with lemon wedges for squeezing over the chicken, accompanied by chunks or slices of crusty bread, if using, for mopping up the juices.

soy chicken wings

ingredients

SERVES 3–4

250 g/9 oz chicken wings,
 defrosted if frozen

250 ml/8 fl oz water

1 tbsp sliced spring onion

2.5-cm/1-inch piece of fresh
 root ginger, cut into
 4 slices

2 tbsp light soy sauce

$^1/_2$ tsp dark soy sauce

1 star anise

1 tsp sugar

method

1 Wash and dry the chicken wings. In a small saucepan, bring the water to the boil, then add the chicken, spring onion and ginger and bring back to the boil.

2 Add the remaining ingredients, then cover and simmer for 30 minutes.

3 Using a slotted spoon, remove the chicken wings from any remaining liquid and serve hot.

mixed leaves with warm chicken livers

ingredients

SERVES 4 AS AN ENTRÉE

250 g/9 oz mixed salad
    leaves, torn into bite-size
    pieces
2 tbsp chopped fresh
    flat-leaf parsley
2 tbsp snipped fresh chives
3–4 tbsp olive oil
100 g/3^1/$_2$ oz shallots,
    finely chopped
1 large garlic clove,
    finely chopped
500 g/1 lb 2 oz chicken
    livers, cored, trimmed
    and halved
3 tbsp raspberry vinegar
salt and pepper
French bread, to serve
    (optional)

method

1 Toss the salad leaves with the parsley and chives and divide between individual plates.

2 Heat 2 tablespoons of the oil in a sauté pan or frying pan over medium–high heat. Add the shallots and garlic and sauté for 2 minutes, or until the shallots are soft, but not brown.

3 Add an extra tablespoon of the oil to the sauté pan and heat. Add the chicken livers and sauté for 5 minutes, or until they appear just pink in the centre when cut in half. Add a little extra oil to the pan while the chicken livers are sautéeing, if necessary.

4 Increase the heat to high, then add the raspberry vinegar and stir quickly. Season with salt and pepper, then spoon the livers and cooking juices over the mixed greens. Serve immediately with French bread, if using.

chicken, cheese & rocket salad

ingredients

SERVES 4

150 g/5$^{1}/_{2}$ oz rocket leaves

2 celery stalks, trimmed
    and sliced

$^{1}/_{2}$ cucumber, sliced

2 spring onions, trimmed
    and sliced

2 tbsp chopped
    fresh parsley

25 g/1 oz walnut pieces

350 g/12 oz boneless roast
    chicken, sliced

125 g/4$^{1}/_{2}$ oz Stilton cheese,
    cubed

handful of seedless
    red grapes, cut in
    half (optional)

salt and pepper

dressing

2 tbsp olive oil

1 tbsp sherry vinegar

1 tsp Dijon mustard

1 tbsp chopped
    mixed herbs

method

1 Wash the rocket leaves, pat dry with kitchen paper and put them into a large salad bowl. Add the celery, cucumber, spring onions, parsley and walnuts and mix together well. Transfer onto a large serving platter. Arrange the chicken slices over the salad, then scatter over the cheese. Add the red grapes, if using. Season well with salt and pepper.

2 To make the dressing, put all the ingredients into a screw-top jar and shake well. Alternatively, put them into a bowl and mix together well. Drizzle the dressing over the salad and serve.

roast chicken salad with orange dressing

ingredients

SERVES 4

250 g/9 oz young spinach
   leaves
handful of fresh parsley leaves
$1/2$ cucumber, thinly sliced
90 g/$3^1/4$ oz walnuts, toasted
   and chopped
350 g/12 oz boneless lean
   roast chicken, thinly sliced
2 red apples
1 tbsp lemon juice
fresh flat-leaf parsley sprigs,
   to garnish
orange wedges, to serve

orange dressing

2 tbsp extra-virgin olive oil
juice of 1 orange
finely grated rind
   of $1/2$ orange
1 tbsp sour cream

method

1 Wash and drain the spinach and parsley leaves, if necessary, then arrange on a large serving platter. Top with the cucumber and walnuts. Arrange the chicken slices on top of the leaves.

2 Core the apples, then cut them in half. Cut each half into slices and brush with the lemon juice to prevent discoloration. Arrange the apple slices over the salad.

3 Place all the dressing ingredients in a screw-top jar, screw on the lid tightly and shake well until thoroughly combined. Drizzle the dressing over the salad, garnish with parsley sprigs and serve immediately with orange wedges.

chicken pinwheels with blue cheese & herbs

ingredients

SERVES 4

2 tbsp pine nuts, lightly toasted

2 tbsp chopped fresh parsley

2 tbsp chopped fresh thyme

1 garlic clove, chopped

1 tbsp grated lemon rind

salt and pepper

4 large, skinless chicken breasts

250 g/9 oz blue cheese, such as Stilton, crumbled

twists of lemon and sprigs of fresh thyme, to garnish

fresh green and red salad leaves, to serve

method

1 Put the pine nuts into a food processor with the parsley, thyme, garlic and lemon rind. Season with salt and pepper.

2 Pound the chicken breasts lightly to flatten them. Spread them on one side with the pine nut mixture, then top with the cheese. Roll them up from one short end to the other, so that the filling is enclosed. Wrap the rolls individually in foil and seal well. Transfer to a steamer, or a metal colander placed over a pan of boiling water, cover tightly and steam for 10–12 minutes, or until cooked through.

3 Arrange the salad leaves on a large serving platter. Remove the chicken from the heat, discard the foil, and cut the chicken rolls into slices. Arrange the slices over the salad leaves, garnish with twists of lemon and sprigs of thyme and serve.

cajun chicken salad

ingredients

SERVES 4

4 skinless, boneless chicken
    breasts, about 140 g/
    5 oz each
4 tsp Cajun seasoning
2 tsp corn oil (optional)
1 ripe mango, peeled, pitted
    and cut into thick slices
200 g/7 oz mixed salad leaves
1 red onion, thinly sliced and
    cut in half
175 g/6 oz cooked beetroot,
    diced
85 g/3 oz radishes, sliced
55 g/2 oz walnut halves
4 tbsp walnut oil
1–2 tsp Dijon mustard
1 tbsp lemon juice
salt and pepper
2 tbsp sesame seeds

method

1 Make 3 diagonal slashes across each chicken breast. Put the chicken into a shallow dish and sprinkle all over with the Cajun seasoning. Cover and chill for at least 30 minutes.

2 When ready to cook, brush a griddle pan with the corn oil, if using. Heat over high heat until very hot and a few drops of water sprinkled into the pan sizzle immediately. Add the chicken and cook for 7–8 minutes on each side, or until thoroughly cooked. If still slightly pink in the centre, cook a little longer. Remove the chicken and set aside.

3 Add the mango slices to the pan and cook for 2 minutes on each side. Remove from the pan and set aside.

4 Meanwhile, arrange the salad leaves in a salad bowl, reserving a few for a garnish, and sprinkle over the onion, beetroot, radishes and walnut halves.

5 Put the walnut oil, mustard, lemon juice, salt and pepper in a screw-top jar and shake until well blended. Pour over the salad and sprinkle with the sesame seeds.

6 Arrange the mango and the salad on a serving plate, top with the chicken breast and garnish with a few of the salad leaves.

san choy bau

ingredients

SERVES 4–6

1 tbsp vegetable or
groundnut oil

100 g/3^1/$_2$ oz chicken, finely
chopped

25 g/1 oz water chestnuts,
finely chopped

1 tsp finely chopped Chinese
chives

25 g/1 oz pine nuts, lightly
toasted

1 tsp salt

^{1}/$_2$ tsp white pepper

6 salad leaves, washed

3 tsp plum sauce, to serve

method

1 In a preheated wok or deep saucepan, heat the oil and stir-fry the chicken for 1 minute. Add the water chestnuts and chives and cook for 2 minutes. Add the pine nuts and cook for 1 minute. Add the salt and pepper and stir.

2 To serve, place a spoonful in the centre of each salad leaf, top with the plum sauce and fold the lettuce leaf to make a small roll.

gingered chicken & vegetable salad

ingredients

SERVES 4

4 skinless, boneless chicken
    breasts
4 spring onions, chopped
2.5-cm/1-inch piece root
    ginger, chopped finely
2 garlic cloves, crushed
2 tbsp vegetable or peanut oil

salad

1 tbsp vegetable or peanut oil
1 onion, sliced
2 garlic cloves, chopped
115 g/4 oz baby corn, halved
115 g/4 oz mangetout, halved
    lengthways
1 red pepper, deseeded
    and sliced
7.5-cm/3-inch piece
    cucumber, peeled,
    deseeded and sliced
4 tbsp Thai soy sauce
1 tbsp jaggery or soft light
    brown sugar
few Thai basil leaves
175 g/6 oz fine egg noodles

method

1 Cut the chicken into large cubes, each about 2.5 cm/1 inch. Mix the spring onions, ginger, garlic and oil together in a shallow dish and add the chicken. Cover and marinate for at least 3 hours. Lift the meat out of the marinade and set aside.

2 To make the salad, heat the oil in a wok or large frying pan and cook the onion for 1–2 minutes before adding the rest of the vegetables, except the cucumber. Cook for 2–3 minutes, until just tender. Add the cucumber, half the soy sauce, the sugar and the basil and mix gently.

3 Meanwhile, soak the noodles for 2–3 minutes (check the packet instructions) or until tender and drain well. Sprinkle the remaining soy sauce over them and arrange on plates. Top with the cooked vegetables.

4 Add a little more oil to the wok, if necessary, and cook the chicken over fairly high heat until browned on all sides. Arrange the chicken cubes on top of the salad and serve hot or warm.

chicken-sesame salad

ingredients

SERVES 4

200 g/7 oz dried thick
    Chinese egg noodles
100 g/3¹/2 oz mangetout
2 celery stalks
4 cooked skinless chicken
    thighs

sesame dressing

3 tbsp dark soy sauce
3 tbsp Chinese sesame paste
¹/2 tbsp bottled hoisin sauce
¹/2 tbsp sugar
¹/2–1 tbsp bottled sweet chilli
    sauce, to taste
1 tsp rice wine
¹/2 tbsp boiling water

method

1 To make the dressing, whisk the soy sauce, sesame paste, hoisin sauce, sugar, chilli sauce and rice wine together, then whisk in the boiling water and continue whisking until the sugar dissolves. Let the dressing stand until it is cool, then cover and chill until required.

2 Meanwhile, cook the noodles in boiling water for 5 minutes (check the packet instructions), until soft. Drain, rinse with cold water to stop the cooking and drain again. Set aside.

3 Use a small, sharp knife to slice the mangetout lengthways into thin strips and cut the celery into thin strips. Use your hands to pull the chicken into thin shreds. If you aren't serving the salad straightaway, cover the chicken and vegetables and let chill.

4 When you are ready to serve, put the noodles, chicken, mangetout and celery in a large bowl. Toss together so all the ingredients are mixed and pour the dressing on top.

red chicken salad

ingredients

SERVES 4

4 boneless chicken breasts

2 tbsp red curry paste

2 tbsp vegetable or peanut oil

1 head Napa cabbage,
    shredded

175 g/6 oz pak choi, torn into
    large pieces

1/2 savoy cabbage, shredded

2 shallots, chopped finely

2 garlic cloves, crushed

1 tbsp rice wine vinegar

2 tbsp sweet chilli sauce

2 tbsp Thai soy sauce

method

1 Slash the flesh of the chicken several times and rub the curry paste into each cut. Cover and chill overnight.

2 Cook in a heavy-based saucepan over medium heat or on a griddle pan for 5–6 minutes, turning once or twice, until cooked through. Keep warm.

3 Heat 1 tablespoon of the oil in a wok or large frying pan and stir-fry the Napa cabbage, pak choi and savoy cabbage until just wilted. Add the remaining oil, shallots and garlic and stir-fry until just tender, but not browned. Add the vinegar, chilli sauce and soy. Remove from the heat.

4 Arrange the leaves on 4 serving plates. Slice the chicken, arrange on the salad greens and drizzle the hot dressing over. Serve immediately.

thai chicken salad

ingredients

SERVES 6

vegetable oil spray

115 g/4 oz skinless chicken
  breast, cut lengthways
  horizontally

3 limes

dressing

1 tbsp finely shredded lemon
  grass

1 small green chilli, finely
  chopped

3 tbsp lime juice

1-cm/^{1}/$_2$-inch galangal or root
  ginger, peeled and thinly
  sliced into strips

1^1/$_2$ tsp sugar

2 tbsp white wine vinegar

3 fl oz water

1^1/$_2$ tsp cornflour

salad

25 g/1 oz rice vermicelli

50 g/1^3/$_4$ oz mixed peppers,
  deseeded

50 g/1^3/$_4$ oz carrot

50 g/1^3/$_4$ oz courgette

50 g/1^3/$_4$ oz mangetout

50 g/1^3/$_4$ oz baby corn

50 g/1^3/$_4$ oz broccoli florets

50 g/1^3/$_4$ oz pak choi

4 tbsp roughly chopped fresh
  coriander leaves

method

1 To make the dressing, put all the dressing
ingredients, except the cornflour, into a small
saucepan over low heat and bring to the boil.
Blend the cornflour with a little cold water,
gradually add to the pan, stirring constantly,
and cook until thickened. Remove from the
heat and let cool.

2 Heat a griddle pan over high heat and spray
lightly with oil. Add the chicken and cook for
2 minutes on each side, or until thoroughly
cooked through. Remove the chicken from
the pan and shred.

3 To make the salad, cover the rice vermicelli
with boiling water then let it cool in the water.
Meanwhile, finely slice the peppers, carrot,
courgette, mangetout and baby corn into
strips. Cut the broccoli florets into 5-mm/^{1}/$_4$-
inch pieces and shred the pak choi. Drain the
rice vermicelli and put all the salad ingredients
with the chicken into a large bowl. Pour over
the dressing and toss together, making sure
that all the ingredients are well coated.

4 Cover and refrigerate for at least 2 hours
before serving. Serve with the juice from half a
lime squeezed over each portion.

lunch
& light meals

Chicken is quick to cook and very easily digested, making it the perfect meat to use for a light lunch or evening meal. One of the fastest and most nutritious options is a stir-fry, which can be prepared and cooked in minutes and served with rice, noodles or a satisfying bread such as naan. Stir-fries are also good because everything goes into the wok, including the vegetables and flavourings, so you only have one pan to deal with – great for all those occasions when you're in a hurry but still want something 'proper' to eat! Try Five-spice Chicken with Vegetables, Sweet-&-Sour Chicken or Chicken with Pak Choi, which is ideal for a low-carb diet.

Curries are also quick to make, and look as if you've put in hours of effort. The Creamy Chicken Curry with Lemon Rice or Balti Chicken are impressive dishes to serve when you have friends coming for a midweek dinner; or give them Chicken Breasts with Coconut Milk, Gingered Chicken Kebabs or Bacon-wrapped Chicken Burgers, all of which can be prepared in advance.

For something a little more exciting than a sandwich, choose Chicken Fajitas or Chicken Tacos from Puebla. If a low-fat recipe is what you're after, Chicken Wraps, Lime Chicken with Mint and Pan-fried Chicken & Coriander are all designed with you in mind!

shredded chicken & mixed mushrooms

ingredients

SERVES 4

2 tbsp vegetable or peanut oil

2 skinless, boneless chicken
    breasts

1 red onion, sliced

2 garlic cloves, chopped finely

2.5-cm/1-inch piece fresh root
    ginger, grated

115 g/4 oz baby white
    mushrooms

115 g/4 oz shiitake
    mushrooms, halved

115 g/4 oz chestnut
    mushrooms, sliced

2–3 tbsp green curry paste

2 tbsp Thai soy sauce

4 tbsp chopped fresh parsley

boiled noodles or rice, to serve

method

1 Heat the oil in a wok and cook the chicken on all sides until lightly browned and cooked through. Remove with a slotted spoon, shred into even-size pieces and set aside.

2 Pour off any excess oil, then stir-fry the onion, garlic and ginger for 1–2 minutes, or until softened. Add all the mushrooms and stir-fry for 2–3 minutes, until they start to brown.

3 Add the curry paste, soy sauce and shredded chicken to the wok and stir-fry for 1–2 minutes. Stir in the parsley and serve immediately with boiled noodles or rice.

five-spice chicken with vegetables

ingredients

SERVES 4

2 tbsp sesame oil

1 garlic clove, chopped

3 spring onions, trimmed
    and sliced

1 tbsp cornflour

2 tbsp rice wine

4 skinless chicken breasts,
    cut into strips

1 tbsp Chinese
    five-spice powder

1 tbsp grated fresh root
    ginger

125 ml/4 fl oz chicken stock

100 g/3$^1/2$ oz baby corn cobs,
    sliced

300 g/10$^1/2$ oz beansprouts

finely chopped spring onions,
    to garnish, optional

freshly cooked jasmine rice,
    to serve

method

1 Heat the oil in a preheated wok or large frying pan. Add the garlic and spring onions and stir-fry over medium–high heat for 1 minute.

2 In a bowl, mix together the cornflour and rice wine, then add the mixture to the pan. Stir-fry for 1 minute, then add the chicken, five-spice powder, ginger and chicken stock and cook for another 4 minutes. Add the corn cobs and cook for 2 minutes, then add the beansprouts and cook for another minute.

3 Remove from the heat, garnish with chopped spring onions, if using, and serve with freshly cooked jasmine rice.

chicken & ginger stir-fry

ingredients

SERVES 4

3 tbsp vegetable oil

700 g/1 lb 9 oz lean skinless,
    boneless chicken breasts,
    cut into 5-cm/2-inch strips

3 garlic cloves, crushed

1 tsp pomegranate
    seeds, crushed

3.5-cm/1$^1/_2$-inch piece
    fresh root ginger, cut
    into strips

$^1/_2$ tsp turmeric

1 tsp garam masala

2 fresh green chillies, sliced

$^1/_2$ tsp salt

4 tbsp lemon juice

grated rind of 1 lemon

6 tbsp chopped fresh
    coriander, plus extra to
    garnish

125 ml/4 fl oz chicken stock

naan bread, to serve

method

1 Heat the oil in a preheated wok or large frying pan. Add the chicken and stir-fry until golden brown all over. Remove from the wok and set aside.

2 Add the garlic, pomegranate seeds and ginger to the wok and stir-fry in the oil for 1 minute, taking care not to let the garlic burn.

3 Stir in the turmeric, garam masala and chillies and fry for 30 seconds.

4 Return the chicken to the wok and add the salt, lemon juice, lemon rind, coriander and stock. Stir the chicken well to make sure it is coated in the sauce.

5 Bring the mixture to the boil, then reduce the heat and simmer for 10–15 minutes, or until the chicken is thoroughly cooked. Garnish with chopped coriander and serve with warm naan bread.

chicken with pak choi

ingredients

SERVES 4

175 g/6 oz broccoli

1 tbsp peanut oil

2.5-cm/1-inch piece fresh
	root ginger, finely grated

1 fresh red Thai chilli,
	deseeded and chopped

2 garlic cloves, crushed

1 red onion, cut into wedges

450 g/1 lb skinless, boneless
	chicken breast, cut into
	thin strips

175 g/6 oz pak choi,
	shredded

115 g/4 oz baby corn, halved

1 tbsp light soy sauce

1 tbsp Thai fish sauce

1 tbsp chopped fresh
	coriander

1 tbsp toasted sesame seeds

method

1 Break the broccoli into small florets and cook in a saucepan of lightly salted boiling water for 3 minutes. Drain and set aside.

2 Heat a wok over high heat until almost smoking, add the oil, then add the ginger, chilli and garlic. Stir-fry for 1 minute. Add the onion and chicken and stir-fry for a further 3–4 minutes, or until the chicken is sealed on all sides.

3 Add the remaining vegetables to the wok, including the broccoli, and stir-fry for 3–4 minutes, or until tender.

4 Add the soy and Thai fish sauces to the wok and stir-fry for a further 1–2 minutes, then serve at once, sprinkled with the coriander and sesame seeds.

chicken satay

ingredients

SERVES 4

2 tbsp vegetable or peanut oil

1 tbsp sesame oil

juice of $^1/_2$ lime

2 skinless, boneless chicken
 breasts, cut into small cubes

dip

2 tbsp vegetable or peanut oil

1 small onion, chopped finely

1 small fresh green chilli,
 deseeded and chopped

1 garlic clove, chopped finely

115 g/4 oz crunchy peanut
 butter

6–8 tbsp water

juice of $^1/_2$ lime

method

1 Combine both the oils and the lime juice in
a non-metallic dish. Add the chicken cubes,
cover with clingfilm and chill for 1 hour. Soak
8–12 wooden skewers in cold water for
30 minutes before use, to prevent burning.

2 To make the dip, heat the oil in a frying pan
and sauté the onion, chilli and garlic over low
heat, stirring occasionally, for about 5 minutes,
until just softened. Add the peanut butter,
water and lime juice and simmer gently,
stirring constantly, until the peanut butter has
softened enough to make a dip – you may
need to add a little extra water to make a
thinner consistency.

3 Meanwhile, drain the chicken cubes and
thread them onto the wooden skewers. Put
under a hot grill or on a barbecue, turning
frequently, for about 10 minutes, until cooked
and browned. Serve hot with the warm dip.

sweet-&-sour chicken

ingredients

SERVES 4–6

450 g/1 lb lean chicken meat, cubed

5 tbsp vegetable or peanut oil

1/2 tsp minced garlic

1/2 tsp finely chopped fresh root ginger

1 green pepper, coarsely chopped

1 onion, coarsely chopped

1 carrot, finely sliced

1 tsp sesame oil

1 tbsp finely chopped spring onion

freshly cooked rice, to serve

marinade

2 tsp light soy sauce

1 tsp Shaoxing rice wine

pinch of white pepper

1/2 tsp salt

dash of sesame oil

sauce

8 tbsp rice vinegar

4 tbsp sugar

2 tsp light soy sauce

6 tbsp tomato ketchup

method

1 Place all the marinade ingredients in a bowl and marinate the chicken pieces for at least 20 minutes.

2 To prepare the sauce, heat the vinegar in a saucepan and add the sugar, light soy sauce and tomato ketchup. Stir to dissolve the sugar, then set aside.

3 In a preheated wok or deep pan, heat 3 tablespoons of the oil and stir-fry the chicken until it starts to turn golden brown. Remove and set aside.

4 In the clean wok or deep saucepan, heat the remaining oil and cook the garlic and ginger until fragrant. Add the vegetables and cook for 2 minutes. Add the chicken and cook for 1 minute. Finally add the sauce and sesame oil, then stir in the spring onion and serve with rice.

chicken with yellow curry sauce

ingredients

SERVES 4

spice paste

6 tbsp yellow curry paste

150 ml/5 fl oz plain yogurt

425 ml//14 fl oz water

handful of fresh coriander,
chopped, plus extra to
garnish

handful of fresh Thai basil
leaves, shredded, plus
extra to garnish

stir-fry

2 tbsp vegetable or peanut oil

2 onions, cut into thin wedges

2 garlic cloves, chopped finely

2 skinless, boneless chicken
breasts, cut into strips

175 g/6 oz baby corn, halved
lengthways

method

1 To make the spice paste, stir-fry the yellow curry paste in a wok for 2–3 minutes, then stir in the yogurt, water and herbs. Bring to the boil, then simmer for 2–3 minutes.

2 Meanwhile, heat the oil in a wok and stir-fry the onions and garlic for 2–3 minutes. Add the chicken and baby corn and stir-fry for 3–4 minutes, until the meat and baby corn are tender.

3 Stir in the spice paste and bring to the boil. Simmer for 2–3 minutes, until heated through. Serve immediately, garnished with the extra coriander and basil.

creamy chicken curry with lemon rice

ingredients

SERVES 4

2 tbsp vegetable oil

4 skinless, boneless chicken breasts, 800 g/1 lb 12 oz in total, cut into 1-inch/ 2.5-cm pieces

1 1/2 tsp cumin seeds

1 large onion, grated

2 fresh green chillies, finely chopped

2 large garlic cloves, grated

1 tbsp grated fresh root ginger

1 tsp ground turmeric

1 tsp ground coriander

1 tsp garam masala

300 ml/10 fl oz coconut milk

250 ml/9 fl oz canned chopped tomatoes

2 tsp lemon juice

salt

2 tbsp chopped fresh coriander, to garnish

lemon rice

350 g/12 oz basmati rice, rinsed

1.25 litres/40 fl oz water

juice and grated rind of 1 lemon

3 cloves

method

1 Heat the oil in a large, heavy-based saucepan over medium heat. Add the chicken and cook for 5–8 minutes, turning frequently, until lightly browned and cooked through. Remove from the pan and set aside. Add the cumin seeds and cook until they start to darken and sizzle. Stir in the onion, partially cover and cook over medium–low heat, stirring frequently, for 10 minutes, or until soft and golden. Add the chillies, garlic, ginger, turmeric, ground coriander and garam masala and cook for 1 minute.

2 Return the chicken to the pan and stir in the coconut milk and tomatoes. Partially cover and cook over medium heat for 15 minutes until the sauce has reduced and thickened. Stir in the lemon juice and season with salt.

3 Meanwhile, put the rice into a saucepan and cover with the water. Add the lemon juice and cloves. Bring to the boil, then reduce the heat, cover and simmer over very low heat for 15 minutes, or until the rice is tender and all the water has been absorbed. Remove the pan from the heat and stir in the lemon rind. Let the rice stand, covered, for 5 minutes.

4 Serve the curry with the lemon rice, sprinkled with fresh coriander.

chicken breasts with coconut milk

ingredients

SERVES 4

1 small onion, chopped

1 fresh green chilli, deseeded and chopped

2.5-cm/1-inch piece fresh root ginger, chopped

2 tsp ground coriander

1 tsp ground cumin

1 tsp fennel seeds

1 tsp ground star anise

1 tsp cardamom seeds

$^1/_2$ tsp ground turmeric

$^1/_2$ tsp black peppercorns

$^1/_2$ tsp ground cloves

625 ml/20 fl oz canned coconut milk

4 skinless, boneless chicken breast portions

vegetable oil, for brushing

fresh coriander sprigs, to garnish

tomato rice and naan bread, to serve

method

1 Place the onion, chilli, ginger, coriander, cumin, fennel seeds, star anise, cardamom seeds, turmeric, peppercorns, cloves and 500 ml/16 fl oz of the coconut milk in a food processor and process to make a paste, adding more coconut milk if necessary.

2 Using a sharp knife, slash the chicken breasts several times and place in a large, shallow, non-metallic dish in a single layer. Pour over half the coconut milk mixture and turn to coat completely. Cover with clingfilm and marinate in the refrigerator for at least 1 hour, and up to 8 hours.

3 Heat a ridged griddle pan and brush lightly with vegetable oil. Add the chicken, in batches if necessary, and cook for 6–7 minutes on each side, or until tender.

4 Meanwhile, pour the remaining coconut milk mixture into a pan and bring to the boil, stirring occasionally. Arrange the chicken in a warmed serving dish, spoon over a little of the coconut sauce, and garnish with coriander sprigs. Serve hot with tomato rice and naan bread.

balti chicken

ingredients

SERVES 6

3 tbsp ghee or vegetable oil

2 large onions, sliced

3 tomatoes, sliced

^{1}/$_2$ tsp kalonji seeds

4 black peppercorns

2 cardamom pods

1 cinnamon stick

1 tsp chilli powder

1 tsp garam masala

1 tsp garlic purée

1 tsp ginger purée

salt

700 g/1 lb 9 oz skinless,
    boneless chicken breasts
    or thighs, diced

2 tbsp plain yogurt

2 tbsp chopped fresh
    coriander, plus extra to
    garnish

2 fresh green chillies,
    deseeded and finely
    chopped

2 tbsp lime juice

naan bread, to serve

method

1 Heat the ghee in a large, heavy-based frying pan. Add the onions and cook over low heat, stirring occasionally, for 10 minutes, or until golden. Add the sliced tomatoes, kalonji seeds, peppercorns, cardamoms, cinnamon stick, chilli powder, garam masala, garlic purée and ginger purée and season with salt. Cook, stirring constantly, for 5 minutes.

2 Add the chicken and cook, stirring constantly, for 5 minutes, or until well coated in the spice paste. Stir in the yogurt. Cover and simmer, stirring occasionally, for 10 minutes.

3 Stir in the chopped coriander, chillies and lime juice. Transfer to a warmed serving dish, sprinkle with more chopped coriander and serve immediately with naan bread.

bang bang chicken

ingredients

SERVES 4

350 g/12 oz boneless,
    skinless chicken meat

few drops of sesame oil

2 tbsp sesame paste

1 tbsp light soy sauce

1 tbsp chicken stock

$^1/_2$ tsp salt

pinch of sugar

8 tbsp shredded lettuce leaves

1 tbsp sesame seeds,
    roasted, to serve

method

1 Place the chicken in a saucepan of cold water, then bring to the boil and simmer for 8–10 minutes. Drain and let cool a little, then cut or tear the chicken into bite-size pieces.

2 Mix together the sesame oil, sesame paste, light soy sauce, chicken stock, salt and sugar and whisk until the sauce is thick and smooth. Toss in the chicken.

3 To serve, put the shredded lettuce on a large plate and spoon the chicken and sauce on top. Sprinkle with the sesame seeds and serve at room temperature.

lime chicken with mint

ingredients

SERVES 6

3 tbsp finely chopped
    fresh mint
4 tbsp honey
4 tbsp lime juice
salt and pepper
12 boneless chicken thighs
mixed salad, to serve

sauce

150 ml/5 fl oz low-fat thick
    plain yogurt
1 tbsp finely chopped
    fresh mint
2 tsp finely grated lime rind

method

1 Mix the mint, honey and lime juice in a
large bowl and season with salt and pepper.
Use cocktail sticks to keep the chicken thighs
in neat shapes and add the chicken to the
marinade, turning to coat evenly.

2 Cover with clingfilm and marinate the
chicken in the refrigerator for at least
30 minutes. Remove the chicken from the
marinade and drain. Set aside the marinade.

3 Preheat the grill to medium. Place the
chicken on a grill rack and cook under the hot
grill for 15–18 minutes, or until the chicken is
tender and the juices run clear when the tip of
a knife is inserted into the thickest part of the
meat, turning the chicken frequently and
basting with the marinade.

4 Meanwhile, combine all the sauce
ingredients in a bowl. Remove the cocktail
sticks and serve the chicken with a mixed
salad and the sauce, for dipping.

bacon-wrapped chicken burgers

ingredients

SERVES 4

450 g/1 lb fresh ground
    chicken
1 onion, grated
2 garlic cloves, crushed
55 g/2 oz pine nuts, toasted
55 g/2 oz Gruyère cheese,
    grated
2 tbsp fresh snipped chives
salt and pepper
2 tbsp wholewheat flour
8 lean Canadian bacon slices
1–2 tbsp corn oil
crusty rolls, chopped lettuce
    and red onion rings,
    to serve
mayonnaise and chopped
    spring onions (green part
    only), to garnish

method

1 Place the ground chicken, onion, garlic, pine nuts, cheese, chives and salt and pepper in a food processor. Using the pulse button, blend the mixture together using short sharp bursts. Scrape out onto a board and shape into 4 even-size burgers. Coat in the flour, then cover and chill for 1 hour.

2 Wrap each burger with 2 bacon slices, securing in place with a wooden cocktail stick.

3 Heat a heavy-based frying pan and add the oil. When hot, add the burgers and cook over medium heat for 5–6 minutes on each side, or until thoroughly cooked through. Serve the burgers at once.

4 Serve the burgers immediately in crusty rolls on a bed of lettuce and red onion rings and topped with mayonnaise and spring onions.

chicken fajitas

ingredients

SERVES 4

3 tbsp olive oil, plus extra
    for drizzling

3 tbsp maple syrup or honey

1 tbsp red wine vinegar

2 garlic cloves, crushed

2 tsp dried oregano

1–2 tsp dried
    red pepper flakes

salt and pepper

4 skinless, boneless
    chicken breasts

2 red peppers, deseeded and
    cut into 2.5-cm/1-inch
    strips

8 flour tortillas, warmed

method

1 Place the oil, maple syrup, vinegar, garlic, oregano, pepper flakes, salt and pepper in a large, shallow plate or bowl and mix together.

2 Slice the chicken across the grain into slices 2.5 cm/1 inch thick. Toss in the marinade until well coated. Cover and chill in the refrigerator for 2–3 hours, turning occasionally.

3 Heat a griddle pan until hot. Lift the chicken slices from the marinade with a slotted spoon, lay on the griddle pan and cook over medium–high heat for 3–4 minutes on each side, or until cooked through. Remove the chicken to a warmed serving plate and keep warm.

4 Add the peppers, skin-side down, to the griddle pan and cook for 2 minutes on each side. Transfer to the serving plate.

5 Serve at once with the warmed tortillas to be used as wraps.

chicken tacos from puebla

ingredients

SERVES 4

8 soft corn tortillas

2 tsp vegetable oil

225–350 g/8–12 oz leftover
    cooked chicken, diced
    or shredded

salt and pepper

225 g/8 oz canned refried
    beans, warmed with
    2 tbsp water to thin

$1/4$ tsp ground cumin

$1/4$ tsp dried oregano

1 avocado, pitted, peeled,
    sliced and tossed with
    lime juice

salsa of your choice

1 canned chipotle chilli in
    adobo marinade,
    chopped, or bottled
    chipotle salsa

175 ml/6 fl oz sour cream

$1/2$ onion, chopped

handful of lettuce leaves

5 radishes, diced

method

1 Heat the tortillas through, in an unoiled non-stick frying pan, in a stack, alternating the tortillas from the top to the bottom so that they warm evenly. Wrap in foil or a clean tea towel to keep them warm.

2 Heat the oil in a frying pan. Add the chicken and heat through. Season with salt and pepper.

3 Combine the warmed refried beans with the cumin and oregano.

4 Spread one tortilla with the refried beans, then top with a spoonful of the chicken, a slice or two of avocado, a little salsa, chipotle to taste, a spoonful of sour cream and a sprinkling of onion, lettuce and radishes. Season with salt and pepper, then roll up as tightly as you can. Repeat with the remaining tortillas and serve at once.

chicken tostadas with green salsa & chipotle

ingredients

SERVES 4–6

6 soft corn tortillas

vegetable oil, for frying

450 g/1 lb skinned, boned
    chicken breast or thigh,
    cut into strips or small
    pieces

250 ml/8 fl oz chicken stock

2 garlic cloves, finely chopped

400 g/14 oz canned
    refried beans

large pinch of ground cumin

225 g/8 oz grated cheese

1 tbsp chopped fresh
    coriander

2 ripe tomatoes, diced

handful of crisp lettuce
    leaves, such as romaine or
    iceberg, shredded

4–6 radishes, diced

3 spring onions, thinly sliced

1 ripe avocado, pitted,
    peeled, diced or sliced,
    and tossed with lime juice

sour cream, to taste

1–2 canned chipotle chillies
    in adobo marinade or
    dried chipotle,
    reconstituted and cut into
    thin strips

method

1 To make the tostadas, fry the tortillas in a small amount of oil in a non-stick frying pan until crisp. Set aside.

2 Place the chicken in a saucepan with the stock and garlic. Bring to the boil, then reduce the heat and cook for 1–2 minutes, or until the chicken begins to turn opaque.

3 Remove the chicken from the heat and let stand in its hot liquid to cook through.

4 Heat the beans in a separate saucepan with enough water to form a smooth purée. Add the cumin and keep warm.

5 Reheat the tostadas under a preheated medium grill, if necessary. Spread the hot beans on the tostadas, then sprinkle with the cheese. Lift the cooked chicken from the liquid and divide between the tostadas. Top with the coriander, tomatoes, lettuce, radishes, spring onions, avocado, sour cream and a few strips of chipotle. Serve at once.

chicken wraps

ingredients

SERVES 4

150 ml/5 fl oz low-fat plain
   yogurt

1 tbsp wholegrain mustard

pepper

280 g/10 oz cooked skinless,
   boneless chicken
   breast, diced

140 g/5 oz iceberg lettuce,
   finely shredded

85 g/3 oz cucumber,
   thinly sliced

2 celery stalks, sliced

85 g/3 oz black seedless
   grapes, halved

8 x 20-cm/8-inch soft flour
   tortillas or 4 x 25-cm/
   10-inch soft flour tortillas

method

1 Combine the yogurt and mustard in a bowl
and season with pepper. Stir in the chicken
and toss until thoroughly coated.

2 Put the lettuce, cucumber, celery and
grapes into a separate bowl and mix well.

3 Fold a tortilla in half and in half again to
make a cone that is easy to hold. Half-fill the
tortilla pocket with the salad mixture and top
with some of the chicken mixture. Repeat with
the remaining tortillas, salad and chicken.
Serve at once.

filo chicken pie

ingredients

SERVES 6–8

1.5 kg/3 lb 5 oz whole
  chicken

1 small onion, halved,
  and 3 large onions,
  chopped finely

1 carrot, sliced thickly

1 celery stalk, sliced thickly

pared rind of 1 lemon

1 bay leaf

10 peppercorns

155 g/5$\frac{1}{2}$ oz butter

55 g/2 oz plain flour

150 ml/5 fl oz milk

salt and pepper

25 g/1 oz kefalotiri or romano
  cheese, grated

3 eggs, beaten

225 g/8 oz filo pastry (work
  with one sheet at a time
  and keep the remaining
  sheets covered with a
  damp tea towel)

method

1 Put the chicken in a large saucepan with the halved onion, carrot, celery, lemon rind, bay leaf and peppercorns. Add cold water to cover and bring to the boil. Cover and simmer for about 1 hour, or until the chicken is cooked.

2 Remove the chicken and set aside to cool. Bring the stock to the boil and boil until reduced to about 625 ml/20 fl oz. Strain and reserve the stock. Cut the cooled chicken into bite-size pieces, discarding the skin and bones.

3 Fry the chopped onions until softened in 55 g/2 oz of the butter. Add the flour and cook gently, stirring, for 1–2 minutes. Gradually stir in the reserved stock and the milk. Bring to the boil, stirring constantly, then simmer for 1–2 minutes until thick and smooth. Remove from the heat, add the chicken and season. Let cool, then stir in the cheese and eggs.

4 Melt the remaining butter and use a little to grease a deep 30 x 20-cm/12 x 8-inch metal baking pan. Cut the pastry sheets in half widthways. Line the pan with one sheet of pastry and brush it with a little melted butter. Repeat with half of the pastry sheets. Spread the filling over the pastry, then top with the remaining pastry sheets, brushing each with butter and tucking down the edges. Bake in a preheated oven, 190°C/375°F/Gas Mark 5, for about 50 minutes, until golden. Serve warm.

green chilli &
chicken chilaquiles

ingredients

SERVES 4–6

12 stale tortillas, cut into
   strips
1 tbsp vegetable oil
1 small cooked chicken, meat
   removed from the bones
   and cut into bite-size
   pieces
salsa verde
3 tbsp chopped fresh
   coriander
1 tsp finely chopped fresh
   oregano or thyme
4 garlic cloves, finely
   chopped
$1/4$ tsp ground cumin
350 g/12 oz grated cheese,
   such as Cheddar,
   Manchego or mozzarella
500 ml/16 fl oz chicken stock
about 115 g/4 oz freshly
   grated Parmesan cheese
375 ml/12 fl oz sour cream
3–5 spring onions, thinly sliced
pickled chillies, to serve

method

1 Place the tortilla strips in a roasting pan, toss with the oil and bake in a preheated oven, 190°C/375°F/Gas Mark 5, for 30 minutes, or until they are crisp and golden.

2 Arrange the chicken pieces in a 23 x 33-cm/ 9 x 13-inch flameproof casserole, then sprinkle with half the salsa, coriander, oregano, garlic, cumin and some of the Cheddar, Manchego or mozzarella cheese. Repeat these layers and top with the tortilla strips. Pour the stock over the top, then sprinkle with the remaining cheese.

3 Bake in the oven at the same temperature for 30 minutes, or until heated through and the cheese is lightly golden in some places.

4 Serve with a dollop of sour cream, sliced spring onions and pickled chillies.

pan-fried chicken & coriander

ingredients

SERVES 4

1 bunch of fresh coriander

1 tbsp corn oil

4 skinless, boneless chicken
breasts, about 115 g/4 oz
each, trimmed of all
visible fat

1 tsp cornflour

1 tbsp water

90 ml/3 fl oz low-fat plain
yogurt

2 tbsp reduced fat light cream

175 ml/6 fl oz chicken stock

2 tbsp lime juice

2 garlic cloves, finely
chopped

1 shallot, finely chopped

1 tomato, peeled, deseeded
and chopped

salt and pepper

method

1 Set aside a few coriander sprigs for a garnish and coarsely chop the remainder. Heat the corn oil in a heavy-based frying pan, add the chicken and cook over medium heat for 5 minutes on each side, or until the juices run clear when the meat is pierced with the tip of a sharp knife. Remove from the pan and keep warm.

2 Mix the cornflour and water until smooth. Stir in the yogurt and cream. Pour the chicken stock and lime juice into the frying pan and add the garlic and shallot. Reduce the heat and simmer for 1 minute. Stir the tomato into the yogurt mixture and stir the mixture into the pan. Season with salt and pepper. Cook, stirring constantly, for 1–2 minutes, or until slightly thickened, but do not let the mixture boil. Stir in the chopped fresh coriander.

3 Place the chicken on a large serving plate, pour the sauce over it and garnish with the reserved coriander sprigs. Serve.

chicken kebabs with yogurt sauce

ingredients

SERVES 4

300 ml/10 fl oz Greek-style
  yogurt

2 garlic cloves, crushed

juice of $1/2$ lemon

1 tbsp chopped fresh herbs
  such as oregano, dill,
  tarragon or parsley

salt and pepper

4 large skinned, boned
  chicken breasts

oil, for oiling

8 firm stems of fresh
  rosemary, optional

shredded romaine lettuce,
  to serve

rice, to serve

lemon wedges, to garnish

method

1 To make the sauce, put the yogurt, garlic, lemon juice, herbs, salt and pepper in a large bowl and mix well together.

2 Cut the chicken breasts into chunks measuring about 4 cm/$1^1/2$ inches square. Add to the yogurt mixture and toss well together until the chicken pieces are coated. Cover and marinate in the refrigerator for about 1 hour. If you are using wooden skewers, soak them in cold water for 30 minutes before use.

3 Preheat the grill. Thread the pieces of chicken onto 8 flat, oiled, metal kebab skewers, wooden skewers or rosemary stems and place on an oiled griddle pan.

4 Cook the kebabs under the grill for about 15 minutes, turning and basting with the remaining marinade occasionally, until lightly browned and tender.

5 Pour the remaining marinade into a saucepan and heat gently but do not boil. Serve the kebabs with shredded lettuce on a bed of rice and garnish with lemon wedges. Accompany with the yogurt sauce.

gingered chicken kebabs

ingredients

SERVES 4

3 skinless, boneless chicken
　　breasts, cut into small
　　cubes

juice of 1 lime

2.5-cm/1-inch piece root
　　ginger, peeled and
　　chopped

1 fresh red chilli, deseeded
　　and sliced

2 tbsp vegetable or peanut oil

1 onion, sliced

2 garlic cloves, chopped

1 aubergine, cut into chunks

2 courgettes, cut into thick
　　slices

1 red pepper, deseeded and
　　cut into squares

2 tbsp red curry paste

2 tbsp Thai soy sauce

1 tsp jaggery or soft light
　　brown sugar

boiled rice, with chopped
　　coriander, to serve

method

1 Put the chicken cubes in a shallow dish.
Mix the lime, ginger and chilli together and
pour over the chicken pieces. Stir gently to
coat. Cover and chill in the refrigerator for
at least 3 hours to marinate.

2 Soak 8–12 wooden skewers in cold water for
30 minutes before use, to prevent burning.

3 Thread the chicken pieces onto the soaked
wooden skewers and cook under a hot grill for
3–4 minutes, turning frequently, until they are
cooked through.

4 Meanwhile, heat the oil in a wok or large
frying pan and sauté the onion and garlic for
1–2 minutes, until softened, but not browned.
Add the aubergine, courgettes and pepper
and cook for 3–4 minutes, until cooked but
still firm. Add the curry paste, soy sauce and
sugar and cook for 1 minute.

5 Serve hot with boiled rice, stirred through
with chopped coriander.

thai-style chicken chunks

ingredients

SERVES 4

4 skinless, boneless chicken
    breasts, cut into small
    chunks
freshly cooked jasmine rice,
    to serve
chopped fresh coriander,
    to garnish

marinade

1 red chilli and 1 green chilli,
    deseeded and finely
    chopped
2 garlic cloves, chopped
50 g/1³/₄ oz chopped fresh
    coriander
1 tbsp finely chopped fresh
    lemon grass
¹/₂ tsp ground turmeric
¹/₂ tsp garam masala
2 tsp brown sugar
2 tbsp Thai fish sauce
1 tbsp lime juice
salt and pepper

method

1 To make the marinade, put the red and
green chillies, garlic, coriander and lemon
grass into a food processor and process until
coarsely chopped. Add the turmeric, garam
masala, sugar, fish sauce and lime juice,
season to taste with salt and pepper and
blend until smooth.

2 Put the chicken chunks into a non-metallic
(glass or ceramic) bowl, which will not react
with acid. Pour over enough marinade to
cover the chicken, then cover with clingfilm
and chill for at least 2¹/₂ hours. Cover the
remaining marinade with clingfilm and chill
until the chicken is ready.

3 When the chicken chunks are thoroughly
marinated, lift them out and barbecue them
over hot coals for 20 minutes, or until cooked
right through, turning them frequently and
basting with the remaining marinade. Arrange
the chicken on serving plates with some
freshly cooked jasmine rice. Garnish with
chopped fresh coriander and serve.

grilled chicken with lemon

ingredients

SERVES 4

4 chicken quarters

grated rind and juice of
    2 lemons

4 tbsp olive oil

2 garlic cloves, crushed

2 sprigs fresh thyme, plus
    extra to garnish

salt and pepper

method

1 Prick the skin of the chicken quarters all over with a fork. Put the chicken pieces in a dish, add the lemon juice, oil, garlic, thyme, salt and pepper, and mix well. Cover and marinate in the refrigerator for at least 2 hours.

2 To cook the chicken, preheat the barbecue or grill. Put the chicken on the barbecue rack or in a griddle pan and baste with the marinade. Cook for 30–40 minutes, basting and turning occasionally, until the chicken is tender. (To test if the chicken is cooked, pierce the thickest part of the chicken pieces with a skewer. If the juices run clear, it is ready.) Serve hot, garnished with thyme sprigs and the grated lemon rind.

hearty
dishes

Although chicken is a light and easily digestible meat, chicken recipes can still be as robust and satisfying as you like. Start with a Traditional Roast Chicken, or Roasted Chicken with Sun-blush Tomato Pesto for a flavoursome variation.

You will find favourite recipes from around the world in this chapter. From France come several classic dishes, including Coq au Vin and Provençal Chicken, both cooked in wine, one of the country's most famous commodities. From neighbouring Italy comes Tuscan Chicken, while Chicken with Goat's Cheese & Basil and Chicken with Walnut Sauce are Greek recipes.

Every meat has its ideal herb, and in the case of chicken, the herb is tarragon. Chicken with Tarragon has a delectable creamy sauce, with a hint of wine and garlic, too. For those who like a little more 'fire' in their flavourings, Red Hot Chilli Chicken and Fiery Chicken Vindaloo really live up to their names.

If keeping your heart healthy is a major consideration, try Sticky Lime Chicken, Chicken with Saffron Mash and Chicken Fricassée. If you are diabetic, Roast Cinnamon Squab Chickens with Spiced Lentils and Spanish Chicken with Preserved Lemons are two recipes especially for you.

traditional roast chicken

ingredients

SERVES 4

25 g/1 oz butter, softened

1 garlic clove,
    finely chopped

3 tbsp finely chopped
    toasted walnuts

1 tbsp chopped
    fresh parsley

salt and pepper

1 oven-ready chicken,
    weighing 1.8 kg/4 lb

1 lime, cut into quarters

2 tbsp vegetable oil

1 tbsp cornflour

2 tbsp water

lime wedges and fresh
    rosemary sprigs,
    to garnish

roast potatoes and a selection
    of freshly cooked
    vegetables, to serve

method

1 Mix 1 tablespoon of the butter with the garlic, walnuts and parsley in a small bowl. Season well with salt and pepper. Loosen the skin from the breast of the chicken without breaking it. Spread the butter mixture evenly between the skin and breast meat. Place the lime quarters inside the body cavity.

2 Pour the oil into a roasting pan. Transfer the chicken to the pan and dot the skin with the remaining butter. Roast in a preheated oven, 190°C/375°F/Gas Mark 5, for 1 3/4 hours, basting occasionally, until the chicken is tender and the juices run clear when a skewer is inserted into the thickest part of the meat. Lift out the chicken and place on a serving platter to rest for 10 minutes.

3 Blend the cornflour with the water, then stir into the juices in the pan. Stir over low heat until thickened, adding more water if necessary. Garnish the chicken with lime wedges and rosemary sprigs. Serve with roast potatoes and a selection of freshly cooked vegetables and spoon over the thickened juices.

roasted chicken with sun-blush tomato pesto

ingredients

SERVES 4

4 skinless, boneless chicken
   breasts, about 800 g/
   1 lb 12 oz in total
1 tbsp olive oil
salt and pepper
2 tbsp pine nuts, lightly
   toasted, to garnish

pesto

125 g/4^1/$_2$ oz sun-blush
   tomatoes in oil (drained
   weight), chopped
2 garlic cloves, crushed
4 tbsp pine nuts,
   lightly toasted
150 ml/5 fl oz extra- virgin
   olive oil

method

1 To make the red pesto, put the sun-blush tomatoes, garlic, 4 tablespoons of the pine nuts and oil into a food processor and process to a coarse paste.

2 Arrange the chicken in a large, ovenproof dish or roasting pan. Brush each breast with the oil, then place a tablespoon of red pesto over each breast. Using the back of a spoon, spread the pesto so that it covers the top of each breast. (Store the remaining pesto in an airtight container in the refrigerator for up to 1 week.)

3 Roast the chicken in a preheated oven, 200°C/400°F/Gas Mark 6, for 30 minutes, or until tender and the juices run clear when a skewer is inserted into the thickest part of the meat.

4 Serve sprinkled with toasted pine nuts.

sticky lime chicken

ingredients

SERVES 4

4 part-boned, skinless
chicken breasts, about
140 g/5 oz each

grated rind and juice of 1 lime

1 tbsp honey

1 tbsp olive oil

1 garlic clove, chopped
(optional)

1 tbsp chopped fresh thyme

pepper

boiled new potatoes and
lightly cooked seasonal
vegetables, to serve

method

1 Arrange the chicken breasts in a shallow roasting pan.

2 Put the lime rind and juice, honey, oil, garlic, if using, and thyme in a small bowl and combine thoroughly. Spoon the mixture evenly over the chicken breasts and season with pepper.

3 Roast the chicken in a preheated oven, 190°C/375°F/Gas Mark 5, basting every 10 minutes, for 35–40 minutes, or until the chicken is tender and the juices run clear when a skewer is inserted into the thickest part of the meat. If the juices still run pink, return the chicken to the oven and cook for a further 5 minutes, then test again. As the chicken cooks, the liquid in the pan thickens to give a tasty, sticky coating.

4 Serve with boiled new potatoes and lightly cooked seasonal vegetables.

roast cinnamon squab chickens with lentils

ingredients

SERVES 4

4 squab chickens, about
500 g/1 lb 2 oz each
2 tbsp maple syrup
1 tsp ground cinnamon
1 tbsp vegetable oil
100 ml/3¹/₂ fl oz low-salt
chicken stock
2 red onions, sliced
1 tsp cumin seeds
1 tsp coriander seeds
1 tbsp olive oil
2 garlic cloves, crushed
800 g/1 lb 12 oz canned
lentils, drained and rinsed
1 tbsp unsalted butter
2 tbsp chopped fresh parsley
pepper
steamed broccoli or green
beans, to serve (optional)

method

1 Arrange the squab chickens in a roasting pan. Mix the maple syrup, cinnamon and vegetable oil together in a small bowl and brush over the breasts of the squab chickens. Pour the stock into the roasting pan and tuck the onion slices around the birds. Roast in a preheated oven, 190°C/375°F/Gas Mark 5, for 35 minutes.

2 Meanwhile, heat a non-stick frying pan over medium heat, add the cumin and coriander seeds and cook, turning, until they start to give off an aroma. Tip into a mortar and finely crush with a pestle.

3 Heat the olive oil in a frying pan over low heat, add the garlic and spices and cook for 1–2 minutes, stirring constantly. Add the lentils to the pan and cook for 10–15 minutes, stirring occasionally.

4 When the birds are cooked, remove from the oven, transfer to a warmed plate, and keep warm. Put the roasting pan on the hob and bring the cooking juices up to a simmer. Stir in the butter and half the parsley and season to taste with pepper.

5 To serve, divide the lentils between 4 warmed serving plates. Add a squab chicken to each plate, pour over the sauce and sprinkle with the remaining parsley. Serve with steamed broccoli or green beans, if liked.

chicken with saffron mash

ingredients

SERVES 4

550 g/1 lb 4 oz floury
    potatoes, cut into chunks

1 garlic clove, peeled

1 tsp saffron threads, crushed

1.25 litres/40 fl oz chicken or
    vegetable stock

4 skinless, boneless chicken
    breasts, trimmed of all
    visible fat

2 tbsp olive oil

1 tbsp lemon juice

1 tbsp chopped fresh thyme

1 tbsp chopped fresh
    coriander

1 tbsp coriander seeds, crushed

100 ml/3½ fl oz hot
    skimmed milk

salt and pepper

fresh thyme sprigs, to garnish

method

1 Put the potatoes, garlic and saffron in a large heavy-based saucepan, add the stock and bring to the boil. Cover and simmer for 20 minutes, or until tender.

2 Meanwhile, brush the chicken breasts all over with half the olive oil and all of the lemon juice. Sprinkle with the fresh thyme and coriander and the crushed coriander seeds. Heat a griddle pan, add the chicken and cook over medium–high heat for 5 minutes on each side, or until the juices run clear when the meat is pierced with the tip of a sharp knife. Alternatively, cook the chicken breasts under a preheated medium-hot grill for 5 minutes on each side, or until cooked through.

3 Drain the potatoes and return the contents of the strainer to the pan. Add the remaining olive oil and the milk, season with salt and pepper and mash until smooth. Divide the saffron mash between 4 large, warmed serving plates, top with a piece of chicken and garnish with a few sprigs of fresh thyme. Serve.

tarragon chicken

ingredients

SERVES 4

4 skinless, boneless chicken
    breasts, about 175 g/
    6 oz each
salt and pepper
125 ml/4 fl oz dry white wine
250–300 ml/8–10 fl oz
    chicken stock
1 garlic clove, finely chopped
1 tbsp dried tarragon
175 ml/6 fl oz double cream
1 tbsp chopped fresh tarragon
fresh tarragon sprigs,
    to garnish

method

1 Season the chicken with salt and pepper and place in a single layer in a large, heavy-based frying pan. Pour in the wine and just enough chicken stock to cover, and add the garlic and dried tarragon. Bring to the boil, reduce the heat and cook gently for 10 minutes, or until the chicken is tender and cooked through.

2 Remove the chicken with a slotted spoon or tongs, cover and keep warm. Strain the poaching liquid into a clean frying pan and skim off any fat from the surface. Bring to the boil and cook for 12–15 minutes, or until reduced by about two-thirds.

3 Stir in the cream, return to the boil and cook until reduced by about half. Stir in the fresh tarragon. Slice the chicken breasts and arrange on warmed plates. Spoon over the sauce, garnish with tarragon sprigs and serve immediately.

tuscan chicken

ingredients

SERVES 4

2 tbsp plain flour

salt and pepper

4 skinned chicken quarters
    or portions

3 tbsp olive oil

1 red onion, chopped

2 garlic cloves, chopped finely

1 red pepper, deseeded and
    chopped

pinch of saffron threads

150 ml/5 fl oz chicken stock
    or a mixture of chicken
    stock and dry white wine

400 g/14 oz canned
    tomatoes, chopped

4 sun-dried tomatoes in oil,
    drained and chopped

225 g/8 oz portobello
    mushrooms, sliced

115 g/4 oz black olives, pitted

4 tbsp lemon juice

fresh basil leaves, to garnish

tagliatelle, fettuccine or
    tagliarini and crusty bread,
    to serve

method

1 Place the flour on a shallow plate and season with salt and pepper. Coat the chicken in the seasoned flour, shaking off any excess. Heat the olive oil in a large, flameproof casserole. Add the chicken and cook over medium heat, turning frequently, for 5–7 minutes, until golden brown. Remove from the casserole and set aside.

2 Add the onion, garlic and red pepper to the casserole, reduce the heat and cook, stirring occasionally, for 5 minutes, until softened. Meanwhile, stir the saffron into the stock.

3 Stir the tomatoes, with the juice from the can, and the sun-dried tomatoes, mushrooms and olives into the casserole and cook, stirring occasionally, for 3 minutes. Pour in the stock and saffron mixture and the lemon juice. Bring to the boil, then return the chicken to the casserole.

4 Cover and cook in a preheated oven, 180°C/350°F/Gas Mark 4, for 1 hour, until the chicken is tender. Garnish with the basil leaves and serve immediately with pasta and crusty bread.

pesto & ricotta chicken

ingredients

SERVES 4

1 tbsp pesto sauce

115 g/4 oz ricotta cheese

4 x 175-g/6-oz skinless,
    boneless chicken breasts

1 tbsp olive oil

pepper

small salad, to garnish

tomato vinaigrette

100 ml/3^1/$_2$ fl oz olive oil

1 bunch fresh chives

500 g/1 lb 2 oz tomatoes,
    peeled, deseeded
    and chopped

juice and finely grated rind
    of 1 lime

salt and pepper

method

1 Mix together the pesto and ricotta in a small bowl until well combined. Using a sharp knife, cut a deep slit in the side of each chicken breast to make a pocket. Spoon the ricotta mixture into the pockets and reshape the chicken breasts to enclose it. Place the chicken on a plate, cover and chill for 30 minutes.

2 To make the vinaigrette, pour the olive oil into a blender or food processor, add the chives and process until smooth. Scrape the mixture into a bowl and stir in the tomatoes, lime juice and lime rind. Season with salt and pepper.

3 Brush the chicken with the olive oil and season with pepper. Cook on a fairly hot barbecue for about 8 minutes on each side, or until cooked through and tender. Transfer to serving plates, spoon over the vinaigrette and serve at once.

chicken rolls with cheese & pine kernels

ingredients

SERVES 6

3 slices white bread, crusts
    removed

6 skinless, boneless chicken
    breasts, about 175 g/
    6 oz each

2 shallots, finely chopped

2 garlic cloves, finely
    chopped

2 tbsp finely chopped fresh
    flat-leaf parsley

2 tbsp freshly grated
    Parmesan cheese

55 g/2 oz pine nuts

pinch of ground mace

salt and pepper

tarragon-flavoured oil or olive
    oil, for brushing

few sprigs of fresh flat-leaf
    parsley, to garnish

method

1 Tear the bread into pieces, place in a bowl and add cold water to cover. Set aside to soak for 10 minutes.

2 Meanwhile, place the chicken breasts between 2 sheets of clingfilm and pound gently with a meat mallet or the side of a rolling pin to flatten.

3 Drain the bread and squeeze out the excess liquid. Mix together the bread, shallots, garlic, parsley, Parmesan, pine nuts and mace in a bowl. Season with salt and pepper.

4 Spread the filling evenly over the chicken breasts and roll up. Secure each roll with a wooden cocktail stick. Brush with the oil and grill, turning frequently and brushing with more oil as necessary, for 25–30 minutes, or until cooked through and tender. Serve at once, garnished with parsley.

chicken with goat's cheese & basil

ingredients

SERVES 4

4 skinned chicken breast fillets

100 g/3$^1/_2$ oz soft goat's
    cheese

small bunch fresh basil

salt and pepper

2 tbsp olive oil

method

1 Using a sharp knife, slit along one long edge of each chicken breast, then carefully open out each breast to make a small pocket. Divide the cheese equally between the pockets and tuck three or four basil leaves in each. Close the openings and season the breasts with salt and pepper.

2 Heat the oil in a frying pan, add the chicken breasts and fry gently for 15–20 minutes, turning several times, until golden and tender.

3 Serve warm, garnished with a sprig of basil.

chicken with walnut sauce

ingredients

SERVES 4

4–8 skinned chicken pieces

$^1/_2$ lemon, cut into wedges

3 tbsp olive oil

150 ml/5 fl oz dry white wine

300 ml/10 fl oz chicken stock

1 bay leaf

salt and pepper

100 g/3$^1/_2$ oz walnut pieces

2 garlic cloves

150 ml/5 fl oz Greek-style
   yogurt

chopped fresh flat-leaf
   parsley, to garnish

rice or pilaf and pitta bread,
   to serve

method

1 Rub the chicken pieces with the lemon. Heat the oil in a large frying pan, add the chicken pieces and fry quickly until lightly browned on all sides.

2 Pour the wine into the pan and bring to the boil. Add the stock, bay leaf, salt and pepper and simmer for about 20 minutes, turning several times, until the chicken is tender.

3 Meanwhile, put the walnuts and garlic in a food processor and blend to form a fairly smooth purée.

4 When the chicken is cooked, transfer to a warmed serving dish and keep warm. Stir the walnut mixture and yogurt into the pan juices and heat gently for about 5 minutes until the sauce is quite thick. (Do not boil or the sauce will curdle.) Season with salt and pepper.

5 Pour the walnut sauce over the chicken pieces and serve hot with rice or pilaf and pitta bread. Garnish with chopped fresh parsley.

chicken tagine

ingredients

SERVES 4

1 tbsp olive oil

1 onion, cut into small wedges

2–4 garlic cloves, sliced

450 g/1 lb skinless, boneless
    chicken breast, diced

1 tsp ground cumin

2 cinnamon sticks, lightly
    bruised

1 tbsp plain
    wholewheat flour

225 g/8 oz aubergine, diced

1 red pepper, deseeded and
    chopped

85 g/3 oz white mushrooms,
    sliced

1 tbsp tomato purée

625 ml/20 fl oz chicken stock

280 g/10 oz canned chickpeas,
    drained and rinsed

55 g/2 oz no-soak dried
    apricots, chopped

salt and pepper

1 tbsp chopped fresh
    coriander

method

1 Heat the oil in a large saucepan over medium heat, add the onion and garlic and cook for 3 minutes, stirring frequently. Add the chicken and cook, stirring constantly, for a further 5 minutes, or until sealed on all sides. Add the cumin and cinnamon sticks to the pan halfway through sealing the chicken.

2 Sprinkle in the flour and cook, stirring constantly, for 2 minutes. Add the aubergine, red pepper and mushrooms and cook for a further 2 minutes, stirring constantly.

3 Blend the tomato purée with the stock, stir into the pan and bring to the boil. Reduce the heat and add the chickpeas and apricots. Cover and simmer for 15–20 minutes, or until the chicken is tender.

4 Season with salt and pepper and serve at once, sprinkled with coriander.

chicken kiev

ingredients

SERVES 4

4 tbsp butter, softened

1 garlic clove, finely chopped

1 tbsp finely chopped fresh
parsley

1 tbsp finely chopped fresh
oregano

salt and pepper

4 skinless, boneless chicken
breasts

85 g/3 oz fresh white or
wholewheat breadcrumbs

3 tbsp freshly grated
Parmesan cheese

1 egg, beaten

250 ml/9 fl oz vegetable oil,
for deep-frying

slices of lemon and flat-leaf
parsley sprigs, to garnish

freshly cooked new potatoes
and selection of cooked
vegetables, to serve

method

1 Place the butter and garlic in a bowl and mix together well. Stir in the chopped herbs and season well with salt and pepper. Pound the chicken breasts to flatten them to an even thickness, then place a tablespoon of herb butter in the centre of each one. Fold in the sides to enclose the butter, then secure with wooden cocktail sticks.

2 Combine the breadcrumbs and grated Parmesan on a plate. Dip the chicken parcels into the beaten egg, then coat in the breadcrumb mixture. Transfer to a plate, cover and chill for 30 minutes. Remove from the refrigerator and coat in the egg and then the breadcrumb mixture for a second time.

3 Pour the oil into a deep-fryer to a depth that will cover the chicken parcels. Heat until it reaches 180–190°C/350–375°F, or until a cube of bread browns in 30 seconds. Transfer the chicken to the hot oil and deep-fry for 5 minutes, or until cooked through. Lift out the chicken and drain on kitchen paper.

4 Divide the chicken between 4 serving plates, garnish with lemon slices and parsley sprigs and serve with new potatoes and a selection of vegetables.

chicken fricassée

ingredients

SERVES 4

1 tbsp plain flour

salt and white pepper

4 skinless, boneless chicken
breasts, about 140 g/5 oz
each, trimmed of all visible
fat and cut into 2-cm/
$3/4$-inch cubes

1 tbsp sunflower or corn oil

8 pearl onions

2 garlic cloves, crushed

250 ml/8 fl oz chicken stock

2 carrots, diced

2 celery stalks, diced

225 g/8 oz frozen peas

1 yellow pepper, deseeded
and diced

115 g/4 oz white mushrooms,
sliced

125 ml/4 fl oz low-fat plain
yogurt

3 tbsp chopped fresh parsley

method

1 Spread out the flour on a dish and season with salt and pepper. Add the chicken and, using your hands, coat in the flour. Heat the oil in a heavy-based saucepan. Add the onions and garlic and cook over low heat, stirring occasionally, for 5 minutes. Add the chicken and cook, stirring, for 10 minutes, or until just beginning to colour.

2 Gradually stir in the stock, then add the carrots, celery and peas. Bring to the boil, then reduce the heat, cover and simmer for 5 minutes. Add the pepper and mushrooms, cover and simmer for a further 10 minutes.

3 Stir in the yogurt and chopped parsley and season with salt and pepper. Cook for 1–2 minutes, or until heated through, then transfer to 4 large, warmed serving plates and serve immediately.

provençal chicken

ingredients

SERVES 4

1.8 kg/4 lb chicken pieces
salt and pepper
1 garlic clove, finely chopped
3 tbsp olive oil
1 onion, finely chopped
225 g/8 oz mushrooms, halved
1 tbsp plain flour
125 ml/4 fl oz chicken stock
175 ml/6 fl oz dry white wine
6 canned anchovy fillets,
    drained
3 tomatoes, peeled, deseeded
    and chopped
2 tsp chopped fresh oregano
6 black olives, pitted

method

1 Rub the chicken pieces all over with salt, pepper and garlic. Heat the oil in a flameproof casserole. Add the chicken and cook over medium heat, turning occasionally, for 8–10 minutes, or until golden. Add the onion, cover and cook over low heat, stirring occasionally, for 20–25 minutes, or until cooked through and tender.

2 Transfer the chicken to a large serving plate, cover and keep warm. Add the mushrooms to the casserole and cook over medium heat, stirring constantly, for 3 minutes. Add the flour and cook, stirring constantly, for 1 minute, then gradually stir in the stock and wine. Bring to the boil and cook, stirring, for 10 minutes, or until thickened.

3 Coarsely chop 4 of the anchovies and add them to the casserole with the tomatoes, oregano and olives, then simmer for 5 minutes. Meanwhile, cut the remaining anchovies in half lengthways. Transfer the sauce and chicken to serving plates, garnish with the halved anchovies and serve at once.

coq au vin

ingredients

SERVES 4

2 tbsp butter
8 baby onions
125 g/4$^{1}/_{2}$ oz bacon,
    roughly chopped
4 chicken joints
1 garlic clove, finely chopped
12 white mushrooms
300 ml/10 fl oz red wine
bouquet garni sachet
1 tbsp chopped fresh tarragon
salt and pepper
2 tsp cornflour
1–2 tbsp cold water
fresh flat-leaf parsley
    sprigs, to garnish
sautéed sliced potatoes,
    to serve

method

1 Melt half of the butter in a large frying pan over medium heat. Add the onions and bacon and cook, stirring, for 3 minutes. Lift out the bacon and onions and reserve.

2 Melt the remaining butter in the pan and add the chicken joints. Cook for 3 minutes, then turn over and cook on the other side for 2 minutes. Drain off some of the chicken fat, then return the bacon and onions to the pan. Add the garlic, mushrooms, red wine, bouquet garni and tarragon. Season with salt and pepper. Cook for about 1 hour, or until the chicken is cooked through.

3 Remove the pan from the heat, lift out the chicken, onions, bacon and mushrooms, transfer them to a serving platter and keep warm. Discard the bouquet garni.

4 Mix the cornflour with enough of the water to make a paste, then stir into the juices in the pan. Bring to the boil, reduce the heat and cook, stirring, for 1 minute. Pour the sauce over the chicken, garnish with parsley sprigs and serve with sautéed sliced potatoes.

spanish chicken with preserved lemons

ingredients

SERVES 4

1 tbsp plain flour

4 chicken quarters, skin on

2 tbsp olive oil

2 garlic cloves, crushed

1 large Spanish onion, thinly sliced

750 ml/24 fl oz low-salt chicken stock

$\frac{1}{2}$ tsp saffron threads

2 yellow peppers, deseeded and cut into chunks

2 preserved lemons, cut into quarters

250 g/9 oz brown basmati rice

white pepper

12 pimiento-stuffed green olives

chopped fresh parsley, to garnish

salad leaves, to serve (optional)

method

1 Put the flour into a large freezer bag. Add the chicken, close the top of the bag and shake to coat with flour.

2 Heat the oil in a large frying pan over low heat, add the garlic and cook for 1 minute, stirring constantly. Add the chicken to the pan and cook over medium heat, turning frequently, for 5 minutes, or until the skin has lightly browned, then remove to a plate. Add the onion to the pan and cook, stirring occasionally, for 10 minutes until soft.

3 Meanwhile, put the stock and saffron into a saucepan over low heat and heat through.

4 Transfer the chicken and onion to a large casserole dish, add the yellow peppers, lemons and rice, then pour over the stock. Mix well and season with pepper.

5 Cover and cook in a preheated oven, 180°C/350°F/Gas Mark 4, for 50 minutes, or until the chicken is cooked through and tender. Reduce the oven temperature to 160°C/325°F/Gas Mark 2$\frac{1}{2}$. Add the olives to the casserole and cook for a further 10 minutes.

6 Serve sprinkled with chopped parsley and accompanied by salad greens, if using.

chicken with yucatan vinegar sauce

ingredients

SERVES 4–6

8 small boned chicken thighs

chicken stock

15–20 garlic cloves, unpeeled

1 tsp coarsely ground
black pepper

1/2 tsp ground cloves

2 tsp crumbled dried oregano
or 1/2 tsp crushed
bay leaves

about 1/2 tsp salt

1 tbsp lime juice

1 tsp cumin seeds, lightly
toasted

1 tbsp plain flour, plus extra
for dredging

125 ml/4 fl oz vegetable oil

3–4 onions, thinly sliced

2 fresh chillies, preferably
mild yellow ones, such as
Mexican Guero or similar
Turkish or Greek chillies,
deseeded and sliced

100 ml/31/2 fl oz cider vinegar
or sherry vinegar

fresh crusty bread, to serve

method

1 Place the chicken in a pan with enough stock to cover. Bring to the boil, then reduce the heat and simmer for 5 minutes. Remove from the heat and let cool in the stock.

2 Meanwhile, roast the garlic in an unoiled frying pan until the cloves are lightly browned on all sides and tender inside. Remove from the heat. Let cool, then squeeze the flesh from the skins into a bowl. Using a mortar and pestle, grind the garlic with the pepper, cloves, oregano, salt, lime juice and three-quarters of the cumin seeds. Mix with the flour.

3 Remove the chicken from the stock, reserving the stock, and pat dry. Rub with two-thirds of the spice paste. Cover and let stand at room temperature for at least 30 minutes.

4 Heat a little of the oil in a frying pan and cook the onions and chillies until golden brown and softened. Pour in the vinegar and remaining cumin seeds, cook for a few minutes, then add the reserved stock and remaining spice paste. Boil, stirring, until reduced in volume.

5 Dredge the chicken in flour. Heat the remaining oil in a heavy-based frying pan. Fry the chicken until lightly browned and the juices run clear when a skewer is inserted into the thickest part. Serve topped with the sauce.

louisiana chicken

ingredients

SERVES 4

5 tbsp corn oil

4 chicken portions

6 tbsp plain flour

1 onion, chopped

2 celery stalks, sliced

1 green pepper, deseeded
    and chopped

2 garlic cloves, finely
    chopped

2 tsp chopped fresh thyme

2 fresh red chillies, deseeded
    and finely chopped

400 g/14 oz canned
    chopped tomatoes

300 ml/10 fl oz chicken stock

salt and pepper

lamb's lettuce and chopped
    fresh thyme, to garnish

method

1 Heat the oil in a large, heavy-based saucepan or flameproof casserole. Add the chicken and cook over medium heat, stirring, for 5–10 minutes, or until golden. Transfer the chicken to a plate with a perforated spoon.

2 Stir the flour into the oil and cook over very low heat, stirring constantly, for 15 minutes, or until light golden. Do not let it burn. Add the onion, celery and green pepper and cook, stirring constantly, for 2 minutes. Add the garlic, thyme and chillies and cook, stirring, for 1 minute.

3 Stir in the tomatoes and their juices, then gradually stir in the stock. Return the chicken pieces to the pan, cover and simmer for 45 minutes, or until the chicken is cooked through and tender. Season with salt and pepper, transfer to warmed serving plates and serve immediately, garnished with lamb's lettuce and a sprinkling of chopped thyme.

red hot chilli chicken

ingredients

SERVES 4

1 tbsp curry paste

2 fresh green chillies, chopped

5 dried red chillies

2 tbsp tomato purée

2 garlic cloves, chopped

1 tsp chilli powder

pinch of sugar

pinch of salt

2 tbsp peanut or corn oil

$^1/_2$ tsp cumin seeds

1 onion, chopped

2 curry leaves

1 tsp ground cumin

1 tsp ground coriander

$^1/_2$ tsp ground turmeric

400 g/14 oz canned chopped tomatoes

150 ml/5 fl oz chicken stock

4 skinless, boneless chicken breasts

1 tsp garam masala

freshly cooked rice and plain yogurt garnished with mint sprigs and diced cucumber

method

1 To make the chilli paste, place the curry paste, fresh and dried chillies, tomato purée, garlic, chilli powder and sugar in a blender or food processor with the salt. Process to a smooth paste.

2 Heat the oil in a large, heavy-based saucepan. Add the cumin seeds and cook over medium heat, stirring constantly, for 2 minutes, or until they begin to pop and release their aroma. Add the onion and curry leaves and cook, stirring, for 5 minutes.

3 Add the chilli paste, cook for 2 minutes, then stir in the ground cumin, coriander and turmeric and cook for a further 2 minutes.

4 Add the tomatoes and their juices and the stock. Bring to the boil, then reduce the heat and simmer for 5 minutes. Add the chicken and garam masala, cover, and simmer gently for 20 minutes, or until the chicken is cooked through and tender. Serve immediately with freshly cooked rice and yogurt garnished with mint sprigs and diced cucumber.

chicken & peanut curry

ingredients

SERVES 4

1 tbsp vegetable or peanut oil

2 red onions, sliced

2 tbsp Penang curry paste

425 ml/14 fl oz coconut milk

150 ml/5 fl oz chicken stock

4 kaffir lime leaves, torn coarsely

1 lemon grass stalk, chopped finely

6 skinless, boneless chicken thighs, chopped

1 tbsp fish sauce

2 tbsp Thai soy sauce

1 tsp jaggery or soft, light brown sugar

50 g/1¾ oz unsalted peanuts, roasted and chopped, plus extra to garnish

175 g/6 oz fresh pineapple, chopped coarsely

15-cm/6-inch piece cucumber, peeled, deseeded and sliced thickly, plus extra to garnish

method

1 Heat the oil in a wok and stir-fry the onions for 1 minute. Add the curry paste and stir-fry for 1–2 minutes.

2 Pour in the coconut milk and stock. Add the lime leaves and lemon grass and simmer for 1 minute. Add the chicken and gradually bring to the boil. Simmer for 8–10 minutes, until the chicken is tender.

3 Stir in the fish sauce, soy sauce and sugar, and simmer for 1–2 minutes. Stir in the peanuts, pineapple and cucumber, and cook for 30 seconds. Serve immediately, sprinkled with the extra nuts and cucumber.

thai red chicken curry

ingredients

SERVES 4

6 garlic cloves, chopped

2 fresh red chillies, chopped

2 tbsp chopped fresh
lemon grass

1 tsp finely grated lime rind

1 tbsp chopped fresh kaffir
lime leaves

1 tbsp Thai red curry paste

1 tbsp coriander seeds,
toasted and crushed

1 tbsp chilli oil

4 skinless, boneless chicken
breasts, sliced

300 ml/10 fl oz coconut milk

300 ml/10 fl oz chicken stock

1 tbsp soy sauce

55 g/2 oz shelled
unsalted peanuts,
toasted and ground

3 spring onions,
diagonally sliced

1 red pepper, deseeded
and sliced

3 Thai aubergines, sliced

2 tbsp chopped fresh Thai
basil or fresh coriander

fresh coriander, to garnish

freshly cooked jasmine rice,
to serve

method

1 Place the garlic, chillies, lemon grass, lime rind, lime leaves, curry paste and coriander seeds in a food processor and process until the mixture is smooth.

2 Heat the oil in a preheated wok or large frying pan over high heat. Add the chicken and the garlic mixture and stir-fry for 5 minutes. Add the coconut milk, stock and soy sauce and bring to the boil. Reduce the heat and cook, stirring, for a further 3 minutes. Stir in the ground peanuts and simmer for 20 minutes.

3 Add the spring onions, pepper and aubergines and simmer, stirring occasionally, for a further 10 minutes. Remove from the heat, stir in the basil and garnish with coriander. Serve immediately with freshly cooked jasmine rice.

green chicken curry

ingredients

SERVES 4

1 tbsp vegetable or peanut oil

1 onion, sliced

1 garlic clove, chopped finely

2–3 tbsp green curry paste

425 ml/14 fl oz coconut milk

150 ml/5 fl oz chicken stock

4 kaffir lime leaves

4 skinless, boneless chicken
   breasts, cut into cubes

1 tbsp fish sauce

2 tbsp Thai soy sauce

grated rind and juice of
   $^1/_2$ lime

1 tsp jaggery or soft light
   brown sugar

4 tbsp chopped fresh
   coriander, to garnish

freshly cooked rice, to serve

method

1 Heat the oil in a wok or large frying pan and stir-fry the onion and garlic for 1–2 minutes, until starting to soften. Add the curry paste and stir-fry for 1–2 minutes.

2 Add the coconut milk, stock and lime leaves, bring to the boil and add the chicken. Reduce the heat and simmer gently for 15–20 minutes, until the chicken is tender.

3 Add the fish sauce, soy sauce, lime rind and juice and sugar. Cook for 2–3 minutes, until the sugar has dissolved. Garnish with chopped coriander and serve immediately, with rice.

fiery chicken vindaloo

ingredients

SERVES 4

1 tsp ground cumin

1 tsp ground cinnamon

2 tsp mustard powder

1 tsp ground coriander

1 tsp cayenne pepper

5 tbsp red wine vinegar

1 tsp brown sugar

150 ml/5 fl oz vegetable oil

8 garlic cloves, crushed

3 red onions, sliced

4 skinless chicken breasts,
    cut into bite-size chunks

2 small red chillies, deseeded
    and chopped

450 g/1 lb potatoes, peeled
    and chopped

800 g/1 lb 12 oz canned
    chopped tomatoes

1 tbsp tomato purée

a few drops of red
    food colouring

salt and pepper

freshly boiled rice, to serve

method

1 Put the cumin, cinnamon, mustard, coriander and cayenne pepper into a bowl. Add the vinegar and sugar and mix well.

2 Heat the oil in a large skillet. Add the garlic and onions and cook, stirring, over medium heat for 5 minutes. Add the chicken and cook for another 3 minutes, then add the chillies, potatoes, chopped tomatoes, tomato purée and a few drops of red food colouring. Stir in the spice mixture, season generously with salt and pepper and bring to the boil. Lower the heat, cover the pan and simmer, stirring occasionally, for 1 hour.

3 Arrange the cooked rice on a large serving platter. Remove the pan from the heat, spoon the chicken mixture over the rice and serve.

chicken pasanda

ingredients

SERVES 4

4 cardamom pods

6 black peppercorns

1/2 cinnamon stick

1/2 tsp cumin seeds

2 tsp garam masala

1 tsp chilli powder

1 tsp grated fresh root ginger

1 garlic clove, very finely
    chopped

4 tbsp thick plain yogurt

pinch of salt

675 g/1 lb 8 oz skinless,
    boneless chicken, diced

5 tbsp peanut oil

2 onions, finely chopped

3 fresh green chillies,
    deseeded and chopped

2 tbsp chopped fresh
    coriander

125 ml/4 fl oz single cream

fresh coriander sprigs,
    to garnish

method

1 Place the cardamom pods in a non-metallic dish with the peppercorns, cinnamon, cumin, garam masala, chilli powder, ginger, garlic, yogurt and salt. Add the chicken pieces and stir well to coat. Cover and marinate in the refrigerator for 2–3 hours.

2 Heat the oil in a preheated wok. Add the onions and cook over low heat, stirring occasionally, for 5 minutes, or until softened, then add the chicken pieces and marinade and cook over medium heat, stirring, for 15 minutes, or until the chicken is cooked through.

3 Stir in the fresh chillies and coriander and pour in the cream. Heat through gently, but do not let it boil. Garnish with fresh coriander and serve immediately.

gong bau chicken

ingredients

SERVES 4

2 boneless chicken breasts, with or without skin, cut into 1-cm/$^1/_2$-inch cubes

1 tbsp vegetable or peanut oil

10 dried red chillies or more, to taste, snipped into 2 or 3 pieces

1 tsp Sichuan peppers

3 garlic cloves, finely sliced

2.5-cm/1-inch piece of fresh root ginger, finely sliced

1 tbsp coarsely chopped spring onion, white part only

85 g/3 oz peanuts, roasted

marinade

2 tsp light soy sauce

1 tsp Shaoxing rice wine

$^1/_2$ tsp sugar

sauce

1 tsp light soy sauce

1 tsp dark soy sauce

1 tsp black Chinese rice vinegar

a few drops of sesame oil

2 tbsp chicken stock

1 tsp sugar

method

1 Combine all the ingredients for the marinade in a bowl and marinate the chicken, covered, for at least 20 minutes. Mix together all the ingredients for the sauce and set aside.

2 In a preheated wok or deep saucepan, heat the oil and stir-fry the chillies and peppers until crisp and fragrant. Toss in the chicken pieces. When they begin to turn white, add the garlic, ginger and spring onion. Stir-fry for about 5 minutes, or until the chicken is cooked.

3 Pour in the sauce, and when everything is well mixed, stir in the peanuts. Serve at once.

noodles & pasta

Noodles and pasta are the busy person's best friend! They are so quick to prepare – noodles often don't even need cooking and can just be soaked in boiling water for a few minutes – and they come in so many shapes and sizes that you never feel that it's 'noodles again' or 'pasta again'! For a really unusual presentation, master the art of making noodle baskets and serve filled with Chicken-Lime Salad or Chicken Chow Mein. If you'd love to try making your own pasta, try Creamy Chicken Ravioli or Chicken Tortellini – you don't need a special machine, and it's very rewarding.

Chicken with Linguine & Artichokes is a delicious option for diabetics. If you have a gluten intolerance, and have sadly concluded that your noodle- and pasta-eating days are over, don't despair – Teriyaki Chicken with Sesame Noodles uses buckwheat noodles which, in spite of their name, are not made from a type of wheat, or try Ginger Chicken with Noodles or Pad Thai, made with rice noodles. Food manufacturers have also responded to the growing number of people with gluten intolerance and produced pastas made from ingredients such as spelt flour or rice, which can be substituted in any of the pasta recipes – follow the cooking instructions on the packet, because they usually cook more quickly than wheat pasta.

teriyaki chicken with sesame noodles

ingredients

SERVES 4

4 boneless chicken breasts,
    about 175 g/6 oz each,
    with or without skin, as
    you wish
about 4 tbsp bottled teriyaki
    sauce
peanut or corn oil
cucumber fans, to garnish

sesame noodles

250 g/9 oz dried thin
    buckwheat noodles
1 tbsp toasted sesame oil
2 tbsp toasted sesame seeds
2 tbsp finely chopped fresh
    parsley
salt and pepper

method

1 Using a sharp knife, score each chicken breast diagonally across 3 times and rub all over with teriyaki sauce. Set aside to marinate for at least 10 minutes.

2 When you are ready to cook the chicken, preheat the grill to high. Bring a saucepan of water to the boil, add the buckwheat noodles and boil for 3 minutes, or according to the packet instructions, until soft. Drain and rinse well in cold water to stop the cooking and remove excess starch, then drain again.

3 Lightly brush the grill rack with oil. Add the chicken breasts, skin-side up, and brush again with a little extra teriyaki sauce. Grill the chicken breasts about 10 cm/4 inches from the heat, brushing occasionally with extra teriyaki sauce, for 15 minutes, or until cooked through and the juices run clear.

4 Meanwhile, heat a wok or large frying pan over high heat. Add the sesame oil and heat until it shimmers. Add the noodles and stir around to heat through, then stir in the sesame seeds and parsley. Season with salt and pepper.

5 To serve, transfer the chicken breasts to plates and add a portion of noodles to each. Garnish with cucumber fans.

sweet-&-sour noodles with chicken

ingredients

SERVES 4

250 g/9 oz dried medium
    Chinese egg noodles
2 tbsp peanut or corn oil
1 onion, thinly sliced
4 boneless chicken thighs,
    skinned and cut into
    thin strips
1 carrot, peeled and cut into
    thin half-moon slices
1 red pepper, cored,
    deseeded and finely
    chopped
100 g/3^1/$_2$ oz canned bamboo
    shoots (drained weight)
75 g/2^3/$_4$ oz cashews

sweet-&-sour sauce

125 ml/4 fl oz water
1^1/$_2$ teaspoons arrowroot
4 tbsp rice vinegar
3 tbsp brown sugar
2 tsp dark soy sauce
2 tsp tomato purée
2 large garlic cloves, very
    finely chopped
1-cm/^{1}/$_2$-inch piece fresh root
    ginger, peeled and very
    finely chopped
pinch of salt

method

1 Cook the noodles in a large saucepan of boiling water for 3 minutes, or according to the packet instructions, until soft. Drain, rinse and drain again, then set aside.

2 Meanwhile, to make the sauce, stir half of the water into the arrowroot and set aside. Stir the remaining sauce ingredients and the remaining water together in a small saucepan and bring to the boil. Stir in the arrowroot mixture and continue boiling until the sauce becomes clear, glossy and thick. Remove from the heat and set aside.

3 Heat a wok or large frying pan over high heat. Add the oil and heat it until it shimmers. Add the onion and stir-fry for 1 minute. Stir in the chicken, carrot and pepper and continue stir-frying for about 3 minutes, or until the chicken is cooked through.

4 Add the bamboo shoots and cashews and stir them round to brown the nuts lightly. Stir the sauce into the wok and heat until it starts to bubble. Add the noodles and use 2 forks to mix them with the chicken and vegetables. Serve immediately.

noodle basket with chicken-lime salad

ingredients

SERVES 4

peanut or corn oil, for
    deep-frying and oiling
250 g/9 oz fresh thin or
    medium Chinese egg
    noodles

chicken-lime salad

6 tbsp sour cream
6 tbsp mayonnaise
2.5-cm/1-inch piece fresh
    root ginger, peeled and
    grated
grated rind and juice of 1 lime
4 skinless, boneless chicken
    thighs, poached and cooled,
    then cut into thin strips
1 carrot, peeled and grated
1 cucumber, cut in half
    lengthways, deseeded
    and sliced
salt and pepper
1 tbsp finely chopped fresh
    coriander
1 tbsp finely chopped
    fresh mint
1 tbsp finely chopped fresh
    parsley
several fresh basil leaves, torn

method

1 To shape noodle baskets, you will need a special set of 2 long-handled wire baskets that clip inside each other, available from gourmet kitchen stores. Dip the larger wire basket in oil, then line it completely and evenly with one-quarter of the tangled noodles. Dip the smaller wire basket in oil, then position it inside the larger basket and clip it into position.

2 Heat 10 cm/4 inches of oil in a wok or deep-fat fryer to 180–190°C/350–375°F, or until a cube of bread browns in 30 seconds. Lower the baskets into the oil and deep-fry for 2–3 minutes, or until the noodles are golden brown. Remove the baskets from the oil and drain on kitchen paper. Unclip the 2 wire baskets and carefully remove the small one. Use a round-bladed knife, if necessary, to prise the noodle basket from the wire frame. Repeat to make 3 more baskets. Let the noodle baskets cool.

3 To make the salad, combine the sour cream, mayonnaise, ginger and lime rind. Gradually add the lime juice until you get the flavour you like. Stir in the chicken, carrot, cucumber, salt and pepper. Cover and let chill. Just before serving, stir in the herbs and spoon the salad into the noodle baskets.

chicken chow mein

ingredients

SERVES 4

250 g/9 oz packet medium
   egg noodles
2 tbsp sunflower oil
280 g/10 oz cooked chicken
   breasts, shredded
1 garlic clove, finely chopped
1 red pepper, deseeded
   and thinly sliced
100 g/3^1/$_2$ oz shiitake
   mushrooms, sliced
6 spring onions, sliced
100 g/3^1/$_2$ oz beansprouts
3 tbsp soy sauce
1 tbsp sesame oil

method

1 Place the egg noodles in a large bowl or dish and break them up slightly. Pour enough boiling water over the noodles to cover and let stand while preparing the other ingredients.

2 Preheat a wok over medium heat. Add the sunflower oil and swirl it around to coat the sides of the wok. When the oil is hot, add the shredded chicken, garlic, pepper, mushrooms, spring onions and beansprouts to the wok and stir-fry for about 5 minutes.

3 Drain the noodles thoroughly then add them to the wok, toss well, and stir-fry for a further 5 minutes. Drizzle the soy sauce and sesame oil over the chow mein and toss until well combined.

4 Transfer the chicken chow mein to warmed serving bowls and serve immediately.

chicken chow mein baskets

ingredients

SERVES 4

6 tbsp water

3 tbsp soy sauce

1 tbsp cornflour

3 tbsp peanut or corn oil

4 boneless chicken thighs,
    skinned and chopped

2.5-cm/1-inch piece fresh
    root ginger, peeled and
    finely chopped

2 large garlic cloves, crushed

2 celery stalks, thinly sliced

100 g/3$^1/_2$ oz white
    mushrooms, wiped
    and thinly sliced

4 noodle baskets made
    with fresh medium
    Chinese egg noodles,
    to serve (see page 162)

method

1 Stir the water and soy sauce into the cornflour in a small bowl and set aside.

2 Heat a wok or large skillet over high heat. Add 2 tablespoons of the oil and heat until it shimmers. Add the chicken and stir-fry for about 3 minutes, or until it is cooked through. Use a slotted spoon to remove the chicken from the wok.

3 Add the remaining oil to the wok, then add the ginger, garlic and celery and stir-fry for 2 minutes. Add the mushrooms and continue stir-frying for a further 2 minutes. Remove the vegetables from the wok and add them to the chicken.

4 Pour the cornflour mixture into the wok and bring to the boil, stirring until it thickens. Return the chicken and vegetables to the wok and reheat in the sauce. Place the noodle baskets on 4 plates and divide the chicken mixture among them.

ginger chicken with noodles

ingredients

SERVES 4

2 tbsp vegetable or peanut oil

1 onion, sliced

2 garlic cloves, chopped finely

5-cm/2-inch piece fresh root
    ginger, sliced thinly

2 carrots, sliced thinly

4 skinless, boneless chicken
    breasts, cut into cubes

300 ml/10 fl oz chicken stock

4 tbsp Thai soy sauce

225 g/8 oz canned bamboo
    shoots, drained and rinsed

75 g/2³/4 oz flat rice noodles

4 spring onions, chopped,
    and 4 tbsp chopped fresh
    coriander, to garnish

method

1 Heat the oil in a wok and stir-fry the onion, garlic, ginger and carrots for 1–2 minutes, until softened. Add the chicken and stir-fry for 3–4 minutes, until the chicken is cooked through and lightly browned.

2 Add the stock, soy sauce, and bamboo shoots to the wok, and gradually bring to the boil. Simmer for 2–3 minutes. Meanwhile, soak the noodles in boiling water for 6–8 minutes. Drain well. Garnish with the spring onions and coriander and serve immediately, with the chicken stir-fry.

pad thai

ingredients

SERVES 4

225 g/8 oz rice noodles

90 g/3¼ oz peanuts, roughly chopped, plus extra to garnish

2 tbsp lime juice

1 tbsp caster sugar

6 tbsp Thai fish sauce

1 tsp hot chilli sauce, or to taste

250 g/9 oz firm tofu (drained weight), cubed

vegetable oil, for deep-frying

3 tbsp peanut oil

1 garlic clove, crushed

1 onion, finely sliced

1 red pepper, deseeded and thinly sliced

250 g/9 oz skinless, boneless chicken breast, cut into thin strips

85 g/3 oz beansprouts

125 g/4½ oz mangetout

175 g/6 oz cooked shelled prawns, cut in half lengthways

3 eggs, beaten

lemon wedges, 4 finely chopped spring onions, and 1 tbsp chopped fresh basil, to garnish

method

1 Soak the noodles in a bowl of warm water for about 20 minutes, or until soft. Drain thoroughly in a colander and set aside. Mix the peanuts, lime juice, sugar, fish sauce and hot chilli sauce together in a small bowl and set aside.

2 Rinse the tofu in cold water, place between layers of kitchen paper and pat dry. Heat the oil for deep-frying in a large frying pan or wok. Deep-fry the tofu over medium heat for 2 minutes until light brown and crisp. Remove from the heat, lift the tofu out with a slotted spoon and drain thoroughly on kitchen paper.

3 Heat another large frying pan or preheated wok and add the peanut oil, garlic, onion, red pepper and chicken strips. Cook for 2–3 minutes. Stir in the beansprouts and mangetout and cook for 1 minute, then add the prawns, noodles, eggs and tofu and stir-fry for 4–5 minutes. Finally, add the peanut and lime juice mixture and cook for 3–4 minutes. Transfer to warmed dishes, garnish with the lemon, spring onions, peanuts and basil and serve immediately.

cross the bridge noodles

ingredients

SERVES 4

300 g/10$\frac{1}{2}$ oz thin egg or
    rice noodles

200 g/7 oz choi sum or
    similar green vegetable

2 litres/64 fl oz chicken stock

1-cm/$\frac{1}{2}$-inch piece of fresh
    root ginger, peeled

1–2 tsp salt

1 tsp sugar

1 boneless, skinless chicken
    breast, finely sliced
    diagonally

200 g/7 oz white fish fillet,
    finely sliced diagonally

1 tbsp light soy sauce

method

1 Cook the noodles according to the directions on the packet. When cooked, rinse under cold water and set aside. Blanch the choi sum in a large saucepan of boiling water for 30 seconds. Rinse under cold water and set aside.

2 In a large saucepan, bring the chicken stock to the boil, then add the ginger, salt and sugar and skim the surface. Add the chicken and cook for about 4 minutes, then add the fish slices and simmer for a further 4 minutes, or until the fish and chicken are cooked through.

3 Add the noodles, choi sum and light soy sauce and bring back to the boil. Test for seasoning. Serve immediately in large individual noodle bowls.

chicken & green vegetables

ingredients

SERVES 4

250 g/9 oz dried medium
  Chinese egg noodles

2 tbsp peanut or corn oil

1 large garlic clove, crushed

1 fresh green chilli, deseeded
  and sliced

1 tbsp Chinese five-spice
  powder

2 skinless, boneless chicken
  breasts, cut into thin strips

2 green peppers, cored,
  deseeded and sliced

115 g/4 oz broccoli, cut into
  small florets

55 g/2 oz green beans,
  trimmed and cut into
  4-cm/1½-inch pieces

5 tbsp vegetable or
  chicken stock

2 tbsp bottled oyster sauce

2 tbsp soy sauce

1 tbsp rice wine or dry sherry

55 g/2 oz beansprouts

method

1 Cook the noodles in a saucepan of boiling water for 4 minutes, or according to the packet instructions, until soft. Drain, rinse and drain again, then set aside.

2 Heat a wok or large frying pan over high heat. Add 1 tablespoon of the oil and heat until it shimmers. Add the garlic, chilli and five-spice powder and stir-fry for about 30 seconds.

3 Add the chicken and stir-fry for 3 minutes, or until it is cooked through. Use a slotted spoon to remove the chicken from the wok and set aside.

4 Add the remaining oil to the wok and heat until it shimmers. Add the peppers, broccoli and beans and stir-fry for about 2 minutes. Stir in the stock, oyster sauce, soy sauce and rice wine and return the chicken to the wok. Continue stir-frying for about 1 minute, until the chicken is reheated and the vegetables are tender, but still firm to the bite. Add the noodles and beansprouts and use 2 forks to mix all the ingredients together.

fettuccine with chicken & onion cream sauce

ingredients

SERVES 4

1 tbsp olive oil

2 tbsp butter

1 garlic clove, chopped
   very finely

4 boneless, skinless chicken
   breasts

salt and pepper

1 onion, chopped finely

1 chicken bouillon cube,
   crumbled

125 ml/4 fl oz water

300 ml/10 fl oz double cream

175 ml/6 fl oz milk

6 spring onions, green part
   included, sliced diagonally

35 g/1¼ oz freshly grated
   Parmesan

450 g/1 lb dried fettuccine

chopped fresh flat-leaf
   parsley, to garnish

fresh crusty bread, to serve

method

1 Heat the oil and butter with the garlic in a large frying pan over medium–low heat. Cook the garlic until just beginning to colour. Add the chicken breasts and raise the heat to medium. Cook for 4–5 minutes on each side, or until the juices are no longer pink. Season with salt and pepper. Remove from the heat. Lift out the chicken breasts, leaving the oil in the pan. Slice the breasts diagonally into thin strips and set aside.

2 Reheat the oil in the pan. Add the onion and gently cook for 5 minutes, or until soft. Add the crumbled bouillon cube and the water. Bring to the boil, then simmer over medium–low heat for 10 minutes. Stir in the cream, milk, spring onions and Parmesan. Simmer until heated through and slightly thickened.

3 Cook the fettucine in boiling salted water until al dente. Drain and transfer to a warm serving dish. Layer the chicken slices over the pasta. Pour on the sauce, then garnish with parsley and serve. Serve with fresh crusty bread.

tagliatelle with creamy chicken & shiitake sauce

ingredients

SERVES 4

25 g/1 oz dried shiitake
    mushrooms

350 ml/12 fl oz hot water

1 tbsp olive oil

6 bacon slices, chopped

3 boneless, skinless chicken
    breasts, sliced into strips

115 g/4 oz fresh shiitake
    mushrooms, sliced

1 small onion, chopped finely

1 tsp fresh oregano or
    marjoram, chopped finely

275 ml/9 fl oz chicken stock

300 ml/10 fl oz whipping
    cream

salt and pepper

450 g/1 lb dried tagliatelle

55 g/2 oz freshly grated
    Parmesan

chopped fresh flat-leaf
    parsley, to garnish

method

1 Put the dried mushrooms in a bowl with the hot water. Let soak for 30 minutes, or until softened. Remove, squeezing excess water back into the bowl. Strain the liquid through a fine-meshed sieve and reserve. Slice the soaked mushrooms, discarding the stems.

2 Heat the oil in a large frying pan over medium heat. Add the bacon and chicken, then stir-fry for about 3 minutes. Add the dried and fresh mushrooms, onion and oregano. Stir-fry for 5–7 minutes, or until soft. Pour in the stock and the mushroom liquid. Bring to the boil, stirring. Simmer for about 10 minutes, continuing to stir, until reduced. Add the cream and simmer for 5 minutes, stirring, until beginning to thicken. Season with salt and pepper. Remove the skillet from the heat and set aside.

3 Cook the pasta until al dente. Drain and transfer to a serving dish. Pour the sauce over the pasta. Add half the Parmesan and mix. Sprinkle with parsley and serve with the remaining Parmesan.

pasta & chicken medley

ingredients

SERVES 2

125–150 g/4^1/$_2$–5^1/$_2$ oz dried
    pasta shapes, such
    as fusilli
2 tbsp mayonnaise
2 tsp bottled pesto sauce
1 tbsp sour cream
salt and pepper
175 g/6 oz cooked skinless,
    boneless chicken
1–2 celery stalks
1 large carrot
125 g/4^1/$_2$ oz black grapes
    (preferably seedless)
celery leaves, to garnish

french dressing

1 tbsp wine vinegar
3 tbsp extra-virgin olive oil
salt and pepper

method

1 To make the french dressing, whisk all the ingredients together in a jug until smooth.

2 Bring a large, heavy-based saucepan of lightly salted water to the boil. Add the pasta, return to the boil and cook for 8–10 minutes, or until just tender but still firm to the bite. Drain thoroughly, rinse and drain again. Transfer to a bowl and mix in 1 tablespoon of the French dressing while hot. Let stand until cold.

3 Mix the mayonnaise, pesto sauce and sour cream together in a bowl, and season with salt and pepper. Cut the chicken into narrow strips. Cut the celery diagonally into narrow slices. Reserve a few grapes for the garnish, halve the rest and remove any pips. Cut the carrot into julienne strips.

4 Add the chicken, celery, carrot, the halved grapes and the mayonnaise mixture to the pasta and toss thoroughly. Taste and adjust the seasoning, if necessary. Arrange the pasta mixture in 2 serving dishes and garnish with the reserved black grapes and the celery leaves.

pappardelle with chicken & porcini

ingredients

SERVES 4

40 g/1½ oz dried porcini
    mushrooms

175 ml/6 fl oz hot water

800 g/1 lb 12 oz canned
    chopped tomatoes

1 fresh red chilli, deseeded
    and finely chopped

3 tbsp olive oil

350 g/12 oz skinless,
    boneless chicken, cut
    into thin strips

2 garlic cloves, finely chopped

350 g/12 oz dried pappardelle

salt and pepper

2 tbsp chopped fresh flat-leaf
    parsley, to garnish

method

1 Place the porcini in a small bowl, add the hot water and soak for 30 minutes. Meanwhile, place the tomatoes and their can juices in a heavy-based saucepan and break them up with a wooden spoon, then stir in the chilli. Bring to the boil, then reduce the heat and simmer, stirring occasionally, for 30 minutes, or until reduced.

2 Remove the mushrooms from their soaking liquid with a slotted spoon, reserving the liquid. Strain the liquid into the tomatoes through a coffee filter paper, or a sieve lined with cheesecloth, and simmer for 15 minutes.

3 Meanwhile, heat 2 tablespoons of the olive oil in a heavy-based frying pan. Add the chicken and cook, stirring frequently, until golden brown all over and tender. Stir in the mushrooms and garlic and cook for a further 5 minutes.

4 While the chicken is cooking, bring a large, heavy-based saucepan of lightly salted water to the boil. Add the pasta, return to the boil and cook for 8–10 minutes, or until tender but still firm to the bite. Drain well, then transfer to a warmed serving dish. Drizzle with the remaining olive oil and toss lightly. Stir the chicken mixture into the tomato sauce, season and spoon onto the pasta. Toss lightly, sprinkle with parsley and serve at once.

spaghetti with parsley chicken

ingredients

SERVES 4

1 tbsp olive oil

thinly pared rind of 1 lemon, cut into julienne strips

1 tsp finely chopped fresh root ginger

1 tsp sugar

salt

250 ml/8 fl oz chicken stock

250 g/9 oz dried spaghetti

4 tbsp butter

225 g/8 oz skinless, boneless chicken breasts, diced

1 red onion, finely chopped

leaves from 2 bunches of flat-leaf parsley

method

1 Heat the olive oil in a heavy-based saucepan. Add the lemon rind and cook over low heat, stirring frequently, for 5 minutes. Stir in the ginger and sugar, season with salt and cook, stirring constantly, for a further 2 minutes. Pour in the chicken stock, bring to the boil, then cook for 5 minutes, or until the liquid has reduced by half.

2 Meanwhile, bring a large heavy-based saucepan of lightly salted water to the boil. Add the pasta, return to the boil and cook for 8–10 minutes, or until tender but still firm to the bite.

3 Meanwhile, melt half the butter in a frying pan. Add the chicken and onion and cook, stirring frequently, for 5 minutes, or until the chicken is light brown all over. Stir in the lemon and ginger mixture and cook for 1 minute. Stir in the parsley leaves and cook, stirring constantly, for a further 3 minutes.

4 Drain the pasta and transfer to a warmed serving dish, then add the remaining butter and toss well. Add the chicken sauce, toss again and serve.

pasta with chicken & feta

ingredients

SERVES 4

2 tbsp olive oil

450 g/1 lb skinless, boneless
    chicken breasts, cut into
    thin strips

6 spring onions, chopped

225 g/8 oz feta cheese, diced

4 tbsp chopped fresh chives

salt and pepper

450 g/1 lb dried garganelli

tomato focaccia, to serve

method

1 Heat the olive oil in a heavy-based frying pan. Add the chicken and cook over medium heat, stirring frequently, for 5–8 minutes, or until golden all over and cooked through. Add the spring onions and cook for 2 minutes. Stir the feta cheese into the pan with half the chives and season with salt and pepper.

2 Meanwhile, bring a large heavy-based saucepan of lightly salted water to the boil. Add the pasta, return to the boil and cook for 8–10 minutes, or until tender but still firm to the bite. Drain well, then transfer to a warmed serving dish.

3 Spoon the chicken mixture onto the pasta, toss lightly and serve immediately, garnished with the remaining chives and accompanied by tomato focaccia.

fruity chicken fusilli

ingredients

SERVES 4

450 g/1 lb skinless, boneless
   chicken, diced

1 tsp ground turmeric

$1/4$ tsp ground cinnamon

$1/4$ tsp ground cumin

$1/4$ tsp ground cardamom

pinch of cayenne pepper

2 tbsp peanut oil

1 onion, finely chopped

2 garlic cloves, finely
   chopped

375 ml/12 fl oz chicken stock

salt

2 tbsp raisins

1 ripe mango, peeled, pitted
   and diced

280 g/10 oz dried fusilli

2 tbsp chopped fresh
   coriander, to garnish

method

1 Place the chicken in a shallow dish. Sprinkle with the turmeric, cinnamon, cumin, cardamom and cayenne and toss well to coat. Cover with clingfilm and let stand in the refrigerator for 30 minutes.

2 Heat the peanut oil in a heavy-based frying pan. Add the onion and garlic and cook over low heat, stirring occasionally, for 5 minutes, or until softened. Add the spiced chicken and cook, stirring frequently, for 5 minutes, or until golden brown all over. Pour in the chicken stock and season with salt. Bring to the boil, add the raisins and mango, partially cover, and simmer for 25 minutes.

3 Meanwhile, bring a large heavy-based saucepan of lightly salted water to the boil. Add the pasta, return to the boil and cook for 8–10 minutes, or until tender but still firm to the bite. Drain and transfer to a warmed serving dish. Add the chicken mixture, toss lightly and serve, garnished with the coriander.

chicken with basil & pine nut pesto

ingredients

SERVES 4

2 tbsp vegetable oil

4 skinless, boneless
   chicken breasts

350 g/12 oz dried fettuccine

pepper

sprig of fresh basil, to garnish

pesto

100 g/3¹/₂ oz shredded
   fresh basil

125 ml/4 fl oz extra-virgin
   olive oil

3 tbsp pine nuts

3 garlic cloves, minced

salt

55 g/2 oz freshly grated
   Parmesan cheese

2 tbsp freshly grated romano
   cheese

method

1 To make the pesto, place the basil, olive oil, pine nuts, garlic and a generous pinch of salt in a food processor or blender and process until smooth. Scrape the mixture into a bowl and stir in the cheeses.

2 Heat the vegetable oil in a frying pan over medium heat. Fry the chicken breasts, turning once, for 8–10 minutes until the juices are no longer pink. Cut into small cubes.

3 Cook the pasta in plenty of lightly salted boiling water until al dente. Drain and transfer to a warmed serving dish. Add the chicken and pesto, then season with pepper. Toss well to mix.

4 Garnish with a basil sprig and serve warm.

chicken with linguine & artichokes

ingredients

SERVES 4

4 chicken breasts, skinned

finely grated rind and juice of
    1 lemon

2 tbsp olive oil

2 garlic cloves, crushed

400 g/14 oz canned artichoke
    hearts, drained and sliced

250 g/9 oz baby plum tomatoes

300 g/10½ oz dried linguine

chopped fresh parsley and
    finely grated Parmesan
    cheese, to garnish

method

1 Put each chicken breast in turn between 2 pieces of clingfilm and bash with a rolling pin to flatten. Put the chicken into a shallow, non-metallic dish with the lemon rind and juice and 1 tablespoon of the oil and turn to coat in the marinade. Cover and marinate in the refrigerator for 30 minutes.

2 Heat the remaining oil in a frying pan over low heat, add the garlic and cook for 1 minute, stirring frequently. Add the artichokes and tomatoes and cook for 5 minutes, stirring occasionally. Add about half the marinade from the chicken and cook over medium heat for a further 5 minutes.

3 Preheat the grill to high. Remove the chicken from the remaining marinade and arrange on the grill pan. Cook the chicken under the preheated grill for 5 minutes each side until thoroughly cooked through. Meanwhile, add the linguine to a saucepan of boiling water and cook for 7–9 minutes, or until just tender.

4 Drain the pasta and return to the pan, pour over the artichoke and tomato mixture and slice in the cooked chicken.

5 Divide between 4 warmed plates and sprinkle over the parsley and cheese.

farfalle with chicken, broccoli & roasted red peppers

ingredients

SERVES 4

4 tbsp olive oil

5 tbsp butter

3 garlic cloves, chopped very
finely

450 g/1 lb boneless, skinless
chicken breasts, diced

$1/4$ tsp dried chilli flakes

salt and pepper

450 g/1 lb small broccoli florets

300 g/$10^1/2$ oz dried farfalle or
fusilli

175 g/6 oz bottled roasted red
peppers, drained
and diced

275 ml/9 fl oz chicken stock

freshly grated Parmesan,
to serve

method

1 Bring a large saucepan of salted water to the boil. Meanwhile, place the olive oil, butter and garlic in a large frying pan over medium–low heat. Cook the garlic until it is just beginning to colour.

2 Add the diced chicken, then raise the heat to medium and stir-fry for 4–5 minutes, or until the chicken is no longer pink. Add the chilli flakes and season with salt and pepper. Remove from the heat.

3 Plunge the broccoli into the boiling water and cook for 2 minutes, or until tender-crisp. Remove with a perforated spoon and set aside. Bring the water back to the boil. Add the pasta and cook until al dente. Drain and add to the chicken mixture in the pan. Add the broccoli and roasted peppers, then pour in the stock. Simmer briskly over medium–high heat, stirring frequently, until most of the liquid has been absorbed.

4 Serve sprinkled with the Parmesan.

chicken tortellini

ingredients

SERVES 4

115 g/4 oz skinless, boneless
chicken breast

55 g/2 oz prosciutto

40 g/1^1/$_2$ oz cooked spinach,
well drained

1 tbsp finely chopped onion

2 tbsp freshly grated
Parmesan cheese

pinch of ground allspice

1 egg, beaten

salt and pepper

double quantity pasta dough
(see page 204)

2 tbsp chopped fresh
flat-leaf parsley, to garnish

sauce

300 ml/10 fl oz single cream

2 garlic cloves, crushed

115 g/4 oz white mushrooms,
thinly sliced

4 tbsp freshly grated
Parmesan cheese

salt and pepper

method

1 Bring a saucepan of lightly salted water to
the boil. Add the chicken and poach for 10
minutes. Let cool slightly, then place in a food
processor with the prosciutto, spinach and
onion and process until finely chopped. Stir in
the Parmesan cheese, allspice and egg and
season with salt and pepper.

2 Thinly roll out the pasta dough and cut into
4–5-cm/1^1/$_2$–2-inch circles. Place ^{1}/$_2$ teaspoon
of the chicken and ham filling in the centre of
each circle. Fold the pieces in half and press
the edges to seal, then wrap each piece
around your index finger, cross over the ends,
and curl the rest of the dough backward to
make a navel shape. Re-roll the trimmings
and repeat until all the dough is used up.

3 Bring a saucepan of salted water to the boil.
Add the tortellini, in batches, return to the boil
and cook for 5 minutes. Drain the tortellini
well and transfer to a serving dish.

4 To make the sauce, bring the cream and
garlic to the boil in a small saucepan, then
simmer for 3 minutes. Add the mushrooms
and half the cheese, season with salt and
pepper and simmer for 2–3 minutes. Pour
the sauce over the tortellini. Sprinkle over the
remaining Parmesan cheese, garnish with the
parsley and serve.

chicken lasagna

ingredients

SERVES 6

2 tbsp olive oil

900 g/2 lb fresh ground
    chicken

1 garlic clove, finely chopped

4 carrots, chopped

4 leeks, sliced

500 ml/16 fl oz chicken stock

2 tbsp tomato purée

salt and pepper

115 g/4 oz Cheddar cheese,
    grated

1 tsp Dijon mustard

625 ml/20 fl oz hot béchamel
    sauce

115 g/4 oz dried no-precook
    lasagna

béchamel sauce

625 ml/20 fl oz milk

1 bay leaf

6 black peppercorns

2 slices of onion

mace blade

4 tbsp butter

6 tbsp plain flour

salt and pepper

wild rocket and Parmesan
    shavings, to serve

method

1 To make the béchamel sauce, pour the
milk into a saucepan and add the bay leaf,
peppercorns, onion and mace. Heat gently to
just below boiling point, then remove from the
heat, cover, infuse for 10 minutes, then strain.
Melt the butter in a separate saucepan.
Sprinkle in the flour and cook over low heat,
stirring constantly, for 1 minute. Gradually stir
in the milk, then bring to the boil and cook,
stirring, until thickened and smooth. Season.

2 Heat the oil in a heavy-based saucepan.
Add the chicken and cook over medium heat,
breaking it up with a wooden spoon, for
5 minutes, or until browned all over. Add the
garlic, carrots and leeks, and cook, stirring
occasionally, for 5 minutes. Stir in the chicken
stock and tomato purée and season with salt
and pepper. Bring to the boil, reduce the heat,
cover and simmer for 30 minutes.

3 Whisk half the Cheddar cheese and the
mustard into the hot béchamel sauce. In a
large ovenproof dish, make alternate layers of
the chicken mixture, lasagna and cheese
sauce, ending with a layer of cheese sauce.
Sprinkle with the remaining Cheddar cheese
and bake in a preheated oven, 190°C/375°F/
Gas Mark 5, for 1 hour, or until golden brown
and bubbling. Serve immediately, with rocket
and Parmesan shavings.

chicken cannelloni

ingredients

SERVES 4

4 skinless, boneless chicken
    breasts, diced

2 tbsp olive oil

6 tbsp butter

550 ml/18 fl oz double cream

1 tsp salt

1 tsp pepper

$^1/_4$ tsp freshly grated nutmeg

55 g/2 oz freshly grated
    Parmesan cheese

450 g/1 lb ricotta cheese

1 egg, lightly beaten

1 tbsp chopped fresh oregano

2 tbsp chopped fresh basil

225 g/8 oz dried cannelloni

75 g/2$^3/_4$ oz mozzarella
    cheese, freshly grated

fresh basil sprigs, to garnish

marinade

100 ml/3 fl oz white wine
    vinegar

1 garlic clove, crushed

275 ml/9 fl oz olive oil

method

1 To make the marinade, mix the vinegar, garlic and olive oil together in a large bowl. Add the chicken, cover with clingfilm and marinate for 30 minutes.

2 Heat the 2 tablespoons of olive oil in a frying pan. Drain the chicken and cook over medium heat for 5–7 minutes, stirring, until no longer pink. Set aside.

3 Melt the butter in a saucepan over medium– high heat. Add the cream, salt, pepper and nutmeg. Stir until thickened. Reduce the heat, add the Parmesan cheese and stir until melted. Remove from the heat.

4 Mix the ricotta, egg and herbs together in a large bowl. Stir in the chicken. Stuff the cannelloni with the chicken mixture. Pour half the sauce into a 23 x 33-cm/9 x 13-inch baking dish. Place the stuffed cannelloni on top. Pour over the remaining sauce. Sprinkle with the mozzarella and cover with foil. Bake in a preheated oven, 180°C/350°F/Gas Mark 4, for 45 minutes. Let stand for 10 minutes before serving, garnished with basil sprigs.

chicken & wild mushroom cannelloni

ingredients

SERVES 4

2 tbsp olive oil

2 garlic cloves, crushed

1 large onion, finely chopped

225 g/8 oz wild mushrooms, sliced

350 g/12 oz ground chicken

115 g/4 oz prosciutto, diced

150 ml/5 fl oz Marsala wine

200 g/7 oz canned chopped tomatoes

1 tbsp shredded fresh basil leaves

2 tbsp tomato purée

salt and pepper

10–12 dried cannelloni tubes

butter, for greasing

625 ml/20 fl oz béchamel sauce (see page 198)

85 g/3 oz freshly grated Parmesan cheese

method

1 Heat the olive oil in a heavy-based frying pan. Add the garlic, onion and mushrooms and cook over low heat, stirring frequently, for 8–10 minutes. Add the ground chicken and prosciutto and cook, stirring frequently, for 12 minutes, or until browned all over. Stir in the Marsala, tomatoes and their can juices, basil and tomato purée and cook for 4 minutes. Season with salt and pepper, then cover and simmer for 30 minutes. Uncover, stir and simmer for 15 minutes.

2 Meanwhile, bring a large, heavy-based saucepan of lightly salted water to the boil. Add the pasta, return to the boil and cook for 8–10 minutes, or until tender but still firm to the bite. Using a slotted spoon, transfer the cannelloni tubes to a plate and pat dry with paper towels.

3 Using a teaspoon, fill the cannelloni tubes with the chicken, prosciutto and mushroom mixture. Transfer them to a large, lightly greased ovenproof dish. Pour the béchamel sauce over them to cover completely and sprinkle with the grated Parmesan cheese.

4 Bake the cannelloni in a preheated oven, 190°C/375°F/Gas Mark 5, for 30 minutes, or until golden brown and bubbling. Serve at once.

creamy chicken ravioli

ingredients

SERVES 4

115 g/4 oz cooked skinless,
    boneless chicken breast,
    coarsely chopped
55 g/2 oz cooked spinach
55 g/2 oz prosciutto, coarsely
    chopped
1 shallot, coarsely chopped
6 tbsp freshly grated romano
    cheese
pinch of freshly grated nutmeg
2 eggs, lightly beaten
salt and pepper
1 quantity basic pasta dough
    (see below)
plain flour, for dusting
300 ml/10 fl oz double cream
    or panna da cucina
2 garlic cloves,
    finely chopped
115 g/4 oz chestnut
    mushrooms, thinly sliced
2 tbsp shredded fresh basil
fresh basil sprigs, to garnish

pasta dough

200 g/7 oz plain flour, plus
    extra for dusting
pinch of salt
2 eggs, lightly beaten
1 tbsp olive oil

method

1 To make the pasta dough, sift the flour into a food processor. Add the salt, eggs and olive oil and process until the dough begins to come together. Knead on a lightly floured board until smooth. Cover and let rest for 30 minutes.

2 Process the chicken, spinach, prosciutto and shallot in a food processor until chopped and blended. Transfer to a bowl, stir in 2 tablespoons of the romano cheese, the nutmeg and half the egg, and season.

3 Halve the pasta dough. Thinly roll out one half on a lightly floured board. Cover with a tea towel and roll out the second half. Place small mounds of the filling in rows 4 cm/1½ inches apart on one sheet of dough and brush in between with beaten egg. Cover with the other half of dough. Press down between the mounds of filling, pushing out any air. Cut into squares and let rest on a floured tea towel for 1 hour.

4 Bring a saucepan of lightly salted water to the boil. Add the ravioli, in batches, return to the boil and cook for 5 minutes. Remove, drain on kitchen paper, then transfer to a warmed dish.

5 Bring the cream to the boil with the garlic in a frying pan. Simmer for 1 minute, then add the mushrooms and 2 tablespoons of the remaining cheese. Season, then simmer for 3 minutes. Stir in the basil, then pour the sauce over the ravioli. Sprinkle with the remaining cheese, garnish with basil sprigs and serve.

rice

Rice dishes are popular the world over, and because different types of rice are produced in various regions, the results are also quite different.

One of the most delicious ways to eat rice is in a risotto. Rice usually needs to be left alone while it's cooking to avoid the starch being released and making the grains stick together but, for a risotto, the plump Italian Arborio rice grains are stirred constantly and explode into a glorious creaminess. Try a simple risotto topped with Chargrilled Chicken Breasts that have been marinated in an olive oil, garlic, lemon and thyme dressing, or Chicken, Mushroom & Cashew Risotto – a delicious combination, just made to go together.

Chicken is one of the key ingredients in a Spanish paella – just the lovely name of Sunshine Paella will give your spirits a boost, before you even start eating the flavourful food! Paellas can be cooked, Spanish-style, on a barbecue.

Rice is consumed in vast quantities in Thailand and China. Egg-fried Rice with Chicken is a Thai classic (remember to allow several hours to let the rice cool completely), while Chicken Steamed with Rice in Lotus Leaves is a stylish Chinese dish.

And for that healthy heart, choose Jambalaya – it's good!

risotto with chargrilled chicken breast

ingredients

SERVES 4

4 boneless chicken breasts,
about 115 g/4 oz each

salt and pepper

grated rind and juice of
1 lemon

5 tbsp olive oil

1 garlic clove, crushed

8 fresh thyme sprigs,
finely chopped

3 tbsp butter

1 small onion, finely chopped

280 g/10 oz Arborio rice

150 ml/5 fl oz dry white wine

1 litre/32 fl oz simmering
chicken stock

85 g/3 oz freshly grated
Parmesan or
Grana Padano cheese

lemon wedges and fresh
thyme sprigs, to garnish

method

1 Place the chicken breasts in a shallow, non-metallic dish and season. Mix together the lemon rind and juice, 4 tablespoons of the olive oil, the garlic and thyme. Spoon over the chicken and rub in. Cover with clingfilm and marinate in the refrigerator for 4–6 hours, then return to room temperature.

2 Preheat a griddle pan over high heat. Cook the chicken, skin-side down, for 10 minutes, or until the skin is crisp and starting to brown. Turn over and brown the underside. Reduce the heat and cook for 10–15 minutes, or until the juices run clear. Let rest on a carving board for 5 minutes, then cut into thick slices.

3 Meanwhile, melt 2 tablespoons of the butter with the remaining oil in a saucepan over medium heat. Cook the onion, stirring occasionally, until soft and starting to turn golden. Reduce the heat, stir in the rice and cook, stirring, for 2–3 minutes, until translucent. Add the wine and cook, stirring, for 1 minute until reduced. Add the hot stock, a ladleful at a time, stirring constantly, until all the liquid is absorbed and the rice is creamy. Season with salt and pepper. Remove from the heat and stir in the remaining butter, then melt in the Parmesan. Serve at once, topped with the chicken slices and garnished with lemon wedges and thyme sprigs.

risotto alla milanese

ingredients

SERVES 4

125 g/4½ oz butter

900 g/2 lb skinless, boneless
   chicken breasts, thinly sliced

1 large onion, chopped

500 g/1 lb 2 oz Arborio rice

150 ml/5 fl oz white wine

1 tsp crushed saffron threads

salt and pepper

625 ml/20 fl oz simmering
   chicken stock

fresh flat-leaf parsley sprigs,
   to garnish

55 g/2 oz Parmesan cheese
   shavings, to serve

method

1 Melt 55 g/2 oz of the butter in a deep frying pan. Add the chicken and onion and cook over medium heat, stirring occasionally, for 8–10 minutes, until golden brown.

2 Reduce the heat, add the rice and cook, stirring constantly, for a few minutes until the grains begin to swell and are thoroughly coated in the butter.

3 Add the wine and saffron and season with salt and pepper. Cook, stirring constantly, until the wine has completely evaporated. Add 2 ladlefuls of the hot stock and cook, stirring constantly, until it has been completely absorbed. Add the remaining stock, 1 ladleful at a time, stirring constantly and allowing each ladleful to be absorbed before adding the next, until all the stock has been absorbed and the rice has a creamy texture – this will take 20–25 minutes.

4 Garnish each individual plate with a parsley sprig, then serve the risotto immediately, sprinkled with the Parmesan cheese shavings and dotted with the remaining butter.

chicken, mushroom & cashew risotto

ingredients

SERVES 4

55 g/2 oz butter

1 onion, chopped

250 g/9 oz skinless, boneless
    chicken breasts, diced

350 g/12 oz Arborio rice

1 tsp ground turmeric

150 ml/5 fl oz white wine

1.4 litres/46 fl oz simmering
    chicken stock

75 g/2³/₄ oz chestnut
    mushrooms, sliced

50 g/1³/₄ oz cashews, halved

salt and pepper

wild rocket, fresh Parmesan
    cheese shavings, and
    fresh basil leaves,
    to garnish

method

1 Melt the butter in a large saucepan over medium heat. Add the onion and cook, stirring occasionally, for 5 minutes, or until softened. Add the chicken and cook, stirring frequently, for a further 5 minutes. Reduce the heat, add the rice and mix to coat in butter. Cook, stirring constantly, for 2–3 minutes, or until the grains are translucent. Stir in the turmeric, then add the wine. Cook, stirring constantly, for 1 minute until reduced.

2 Gradually add the hot stock, a ladleful at a time. Stir constantly and add more liquid as the rice absorbs each addition. Increase the heat to medium so that the liquid bubbles. Cook for 20 minutes, or until all the liquid is absorbed and the rice is creamy. About 3 minutes before the end of the cooking time, stir in the mushrooms and cashews. Season with salt and pepper.

3 Arrange the rocket leaves on 4 individual serving plates. Remove the risotto from the heat and spoon it over the rocket. Sprinkle over the Parmesan shavings and basil leaves and serve.

chicken risotto with saffron

ingredients

SERVES 4

125 g/4¹/₂ oz butter

900 g/2 lb skinless, boneless
   chicken breasts,
   thinly sliced

1 large onion, chopped

500 g/1 lb 2 oz Arborio rice

150 ml/5 fl oz white wine

1 tsp crumbled saffron threads

1.4 litres/46 fl oz simmering
   chicken stock

salt and pepper

55 g/2 oz freshly grated
   Parmesan cheese

method

1 Heat 55 g/2 oz of the butter in a deep
saucepan, add the chicken and onion and
cook, stirring frequently, for 8 minutes, or until
golden brown. Add the rice and mix to coat in
the butter. Cook, stirring constantly for 2–3
minutes, or until the grains are translucent.
Add the wine and cook, stirring constantly, for
1 minute until reduced.

2 Mix the saffron with 4 tablespoons of the
hot stock. Add the liquid to the rice and cook,
stirring constantly, until it is absorbed.
Gradually add the remaining hot stock, a
ladleful at a time. Stir constantly and add
more liquid as the rice absorbs each addition.
Cook for 20 minutes, or until all the liquid is
absorbed and the rice is creamy. Season with
salt and pepper.

3 Remove the risotto from the heat and add
the remaining butter. Mix well, then stir in the
Parmesan until it melts. Spoon the risotto
onto warmed plates and serve at once.

sunshine paella

ingredients

SERVES 4–6

$^1/_2$ tsp saffron threads

2 tbsp hot water

150 g/5$^1/_2$ oz cod, rinsed

1.4 litres/46 fl oz simmering
    fish stock

12 large raw prawns, shelled
    and deveined

200 g/7 oz live mussels,
    scrubbed and debearded

3 tbsp olive oil

150 g/5$^1/_2$ oz chicken breast,
    cut into bite-size chunks
    and seasoned to taste

1 large red onion, chopped

2 garlic cloves, chopped

$^1/_2$ tsp cayenne pepper

$^1/_2$ tsp paprika

225 g/8 oz tomatoes, peeled
    and cut into wedges

1 red pepper and 1 yellow
    pepper, deseeded and
    sliced

375 g/13 oz paella rice

salt and pepper

175 g/6 oz canned sweetcorn
    kernels, drained

3 hard-boiled eggs, cut into
    quarters lengthways,
    to serve

lemon wedges, to serve

method

1 Put the saffron threads and water in a bowl and infuse. Cook the cod in the simmering stock for 5 minutes. Rinse under cold running water, drain, cut into chunks and set aside in a bowl. Cook the prawns in the stock for 2 minutes. Add to the cod. Discard any mussels with broken shells or that refuse to close when tapped. Add to the stock and cook until opened. Add to the bowl with the other seafood, discarding any that remain closed.

2 Heat the oil in a paella pan over medium heat. Cook the chicken, stirring, for 5 minutes. Add the onion and cook, stirring, until softened. Add the garlic, cayenne pepper, paprika and saffron and its soaking liquid and cook, stirring, for 1 minute. Add the tomatoes and peppers and cook, stirring, for 2 minutes.

3 Add the rice and cook, stirring, for 1 minute. Add most of the stock, bring to the boil, then simmer, uncovered, for 10 minutes. Do not stir during cooking, but shake the pan once or twice and when adding ingredients. Season, then cook for 10 minutes, or until the rice is almost cooked, adding more stock if necessary. Add the seafood and corn and cook for 3 minutes.

4 When all the liquid has been absorbed and you detect a faint toasty aroma coming from the rice, remove from the heat. Cover with foil and stand for 5 minutes. Serve topped with egg quarters and garnished with lemon wedges.

chicken & prawn paella

ingredients

SERVES 6–8

$^1/_2$ tsp saffron threads

2 tbsp hot water

about 6 tbsp olive oil

6–8 chicken thighs (on the
bone, skin on), excess fat
removed

140 g/5 oz Spanish chorizo
sausage, casing removed,
cut into 5-mm/$^1/_4$-inch slices

2 large onions, chopped

4 large garlic cloves, crushed

1 tsp mild or hot Spanish
paprika, to taste

375 g/13 oz medium-grain
paella rice

100 g/3$^1/_2$ oz green beans,
chopped

85 g/3 oz frozen peas

1.25 litres/40 fl oz
chicken stock

salt and pepper

16 live mussels, scrubbed and
debearded (discard any
that refuse to close)

16 raw prawns, shelled and
deveined

2 red peppers, grilled, peeled,
deseeded and sliced

35 g/1$^1/_4$ oz fresh parsley,
chopped, to garnish

method

1 Put the saffron threads and water in a small bowl and infuse for a few minutes.

2 Heat 3 tablespoons of the oil in a 30-cm/ 12-inch paella pan. Cook the chicken thighs over medium–high heat, turning frequently, for 5 minutes, or until golden and crispy. Transfer to a bowl. Add the chorizo to the pan and cook, stirring, for 1 minute, or until beginning to crisp. Add to the chicken.

3 Heat another 3 tablespoons of the oil in the pan and cook the onions, stirring frequently, for 2 minutes, then add the garlic and paprika and cook, stirring, for 3 minutes, or until the onions are soft, but not browned. Add the drained rice, beans and peas and stir until coated in oil. Return the chicken, chorizo and any juices to the pan. Stir in the stock and the saffron with its soaking liquid, and season with salt and pepper. Bring to the boil, stirring constantly, then simmer, uncovered and without stirring, for 15 minutes, or until the rice is almost tender and most of the liquid has been absorbed.

4 Arrange the mussels, prawns and red pepper slices on top, then cover and simmer, without stirring, for 5 minutes, or until the prawns turn pink and the mussels open. Discard any mussels that remain closed. Serve at once, sprinkled with the parsley.

chicken & duck paella with orange

ingredients

SERVES 4–6

1/2 tsp saffron threads

2 tbsp hot water

175 g/6 oz skinless, boneless
    chicken breast

4 large skinless, boneless
    duck breasts

salt and pepper

2 tbsp olive oil

1 large onion, chopped

2 garlic cloves, crushed

1 tsp paprika

225 g/8 oz tomato wedges

1 orange pepper, grilled,
    peeled, deseeded and
    chopped

175 g/6 oz canned red kidney
    beans (drained weight)

375 g/13 oz paella rice

1 tbsp chopped fresh flat-leaf
    parsley, plus extra sprigs
    to garnish

1 tbsp freshly grated
    orange rind

2 tbsp orange juice

100 ml/3 1/2 fl oz white wine

1.25 litres/40 fl oz simmering
    chicken stock

orange wedges, to garnish

method

1 Put the saffron threads and water in a small bowl and infuse for a few minutes.

2 Cut the chicken and duck into bite-size chunks and season. Heat the oil in a paella pan and cook the chicken and duck over medium–high heat, stirring, until golden all over. Transfer to a bowl and set aside.

3 Add the onion and cook over medium heat, stirring, until softened. Add the garlic, paprika and saffron and its soaking liquid and cook, stirring constantly, for 1 minute. Add the tomato wedges, orange pepper and beans and cook, stirring, for a further 2 minutes.

4 Add the rice and parsley and cook, stirring, for 1 minute. Add the orange rind and juice, the wine and most of the hot stock. Bring to the boil, then simmer, uncovered, for 10 minutes. Do not stir during cooking, but shake the pan once or twice, and when adding ingredients. Return the chicken and duck to the pan and season. Cook for 10–15 minutes, or until the rice grains are plump and cooked, adding a little more stock if necessary.

5 When all the liquid has been absorbed and you detect a faint toasty aroma coming from the rice, remove from the heat. Cover with foil and stand for 5 minutes. Garnish with parsley sprigs and orange wedges to serve.

paella with pork & chorizo

ingredients

SERVES 4–6

1.25 litres/40 fl oz simmering
   fish stock

12 large raw prawns, in their
   shells

$^{1}/_{2}$ tsp saffron threads

2 tbsp hot water

100 g/3$^{1}/_{2}$ oz skinless,
   boneless chicken breast,
   cut into 1-cm/$^{1}/_{2}$-inch
   pieces

100 g/3$^{1}/_{2}$ oz pork tenderloin,
   cut into 1-cm/$^{1}/_{2}$-inch
   pieces

salt and pepper

3 tbsp olive oil

100 g/3$^{1}/_{2}$ oz Spanish chorizo
   sausage, casing removed,
   cut into 1-cm/$^{1}/_{2}$-inch
   slices

1 large red onion, chopped

2 garlic cloves, crushed

$^{1}/_{2}$ tsp cayenne pepper

$^{1}/_{2}$ tsp paprika

1 red pepper, deseeded
   and sliced

1 green pepper, deseeded
   and sliced

12 cherry tomatoes, halved

375 g/13 oz paella rice

1 tbsp chopped fresh parsley

2 tsp chopped fresh tarragon

method

1 Add the prawns to the simmering stock and cook for 2 minutes, then transfer to a bowl and set aside. Put the saffron threads and water in a small bowl and infuse for a few minutes.

2 Season the chicken and pork with salt and pepper. Heat the oil in a paella pan and cook the chicken, pork and chorizo over medium heat, stirring, until golden. Add the onion and cook, stirring, until softened. Add the garlic, cayenne pepper, paprika and saffron and its soaking liquid and cook, stirring constantly, for 1 minute. Add the peppers and tomatoes and cook, stirring, for a further 2 minutes.

3 Add the rice and herbs and cook, stirring constantly, for 1 minute. Pour in most of the hot stock, bring to the boil, then simmer, uncovered, for 10 minutes. Do not stir during cooking, but shake the pan once or twice and when adding ingredients. Season, then cook for a further 10 minutes, or until the rice is almost cooked, adding a little more hot stock if necessary. Add the prawns and cook for a further 2 minutes.

4 When all the liquid has been absorbed and you detect a faint toasty aroma coming from the rice, remove from the heat. Cover with foil and stand for 5 minutes. Serve.

spanish rice with chicken

ingredients

SERVES 4

3 tbsp olive oil

1.25 kg/2 lb 12 oz chicken
    pieces

salt and pepper

2 onions, sliced

175 g/6 oz long-grain rice

125 ml/4 fl oz dry white wine

pinch of saffron threads,
    lightly crushed

375 ml/12 fl oz chicken stock

1–2 mild fresh green chillies,
    such as serrano

2 garlic cloves, finely
    chopped

2 beefsteak tomatoes, peeled,
    deseeded and chopped

fresh coriander sprigs,
    to garnish

method

1 Heat 2 tablespoons of the oil in a flameproof casserole. Season the chicken with salt and pepper, add to the casserole and cook over medium heat, turning occasionally, for 8–10 minutes, or until golden. Transfer to a plate with a perforated spoon.

2 Add the remaining oil to the casserole. Add the onions and cook over low heat, stirring occasionally, for 5 minutes, or until translucent. Add the rice and cook, stirring, for 2 minutes, or until the grains are transparent and coated with oil.

3 Pour in the wine. Bring to the boil, then reduce the heat, cover and simmer for 8 minutes, or until all the liquid has been absorbed. Combine the saffron and stock and pour into the casserole. Stir in the chillies and garlic and season with salt. Cover and simmer for 15 minutes.

4 Add the tomatoes and return the chicken pieces to the casserole, pushing them down into the rice. Cover and cook for a further 25 minutes, or until the chicken is cooked through and tender. Garnish with coriander sprigs and serve.

greek chicken with rice

ingredients

SERVES 4

8 chicken thighs

2 tbsp corn oil

1 onion, chopped

2 garlic cloves, finely chopped

175 g/6 oz long-grain rice

225 ml/7 fl oz chicken stock

800 g/1 lb 12 oz canned
    chopped tomatoes

1 tbsp chopped fresh thyme

2 tbsp chopped fresh oregano

12 black olives, pitted and
    chopped

55 g/2 oz feta cheese,
    crumbled

fresh oregano sprigs, to garnish

method

1 Remove the skin from the chicken. Heat the oil in a flameproof casserole. Add the chicken, in batches, if necessary, and cook over medium heat, turning occasionally, for 8–10 minutes, or until golden. Transfer to a plate with a perforated spoon.

2 Add the onion, garlic, rice and 50 ml/2 fl oz of the stock to the casserole and cook, stirring, for 5 minutes, or until the onion is softened. Pour in the remaining stock and add the tomatoes and their juices and the herbs.

3 Return the chicken thighs to the casserole, pushing them down into the rice. Bring to the boil, then reduce the heat, cover and simmer for 25–30 minutes, or until the chicken is cooked through and tender. Stir in the olives and sprinkle the cheese on top. Garnish with oregano sprigs and serve immediately.

jambalaya

ingredients

SERVES 4

400 g/14 oz skinless, boneless
   chicken breast, diced
1 red onion, diced
1 garlic clove, crushed
625 ml/20 fl oz chicken stock
400 g/14 oz canned chopped
   tomatoes in tomato juice
280 g/10 oz brown rice
1–2 tsp hot chilli powder
1/2 tsp paprika
1 tsp dried oregano
1 red pepper, deseeded
   and diced
1 yellow pepper, deseeded
   and diced
85 g/3 oz frozen
   sweetcorn kernels
85 g/3 oz frozen peas
3 tbsp chopped fresh parsley
pepper
crisp salad leaves, to serve
   (optional)

method

1 Put the chicken, onion, garlic, stock,
tomatoes and rice into a large, heavy-based
saucepan. Add the chilli powder, paprika and
oregano and stir well. Bring to the boil, then
reduce the heat, cover and simmer for
25 minutes.

2 Add the red and yellow peppers, sweetcorn
and peas to the rice mixture and return to the
boil. Reduce the heat, cover and simmer for a
further 10 minutes, or until the rice is just
tender (brown rice retains a 'nutty' texture
when cooked) and most of the stock has been
absorbed but is not completely dry.

3 Stir in 2 tablespoons of the parsley and
season with pepper. Transfer the jambalaya
to a warmed serving dish, garnish with the
remaining parsley, and serve with crisp
salad leaves, if using.

egg-fried rice with chicken

ingredients

SERVES 4

225 g/8 oz jasmine rice

3 skinless, boneless chicken
   breasts, cut into cubes

400 ml/14 fl oz canned
   coconut milk

50 g/1³/₄ oz block creamed
   coconut, chopped

2–3 coriander roots, chopped

thinly pared rind of 1 lemon

1 fresh green chilli, deseeded
   and chopped

3 fresh Thai basil leaves

1 tbsp fish sauce

1 tbsp oil

3 eggs, beaten

fresh chives and sprigs fresh
   coriander, to garnish

method

1 Cook the rice in boiling water for 12–15 minutes, drain well, then cool and chill overnight.

2 Put the chicken into a saucepan and cover with the coconut milk. Add the creamed coconut, coriander roots, lemon rind and chilli and bring to the boil. Simmer for 8–10 minutes, until the chicken is tender. Remove from the heat. Stir in the basil and fish sauce.

3 Meanwhile, heat the oil in a wok and stir-fry the rice for 2–3 minutes. Pour in the eggs and stir until they have cooked and mixed with the rice. Line 4 small ovenproof bowls or ramekins with clingfilm and pack with the rice. Turn out carefully onto serving plates and remove the clingfilm. Garnish with long chives and sprigs of coriander. Serve with the chicken.

hainan chicken rice

ingredients

SERVES 4–6

1 chicken, weighing
    1.5 kg/3 lb 5 oz
55 g/2 oz fresh young root
    ginger, smashed
2 garlic cloves, smashed
1 spring onion, tied in a knot
1 tsp salt
2 tbsp vegetable or peanut oil
chilli or soy dipping sauce,
    to serve

rice

2 tbsp vegetable or peanut oil
5 garlic cloves, finely chopped
5 shallots, finely chopped
350 g/12 oz long-grain rice
950 ml/30 fl oz chicken stock
1 tsp salt

method

1 Wash the chicken and dry thoroughly. Stuff the body cavity with the ginger, garlic, spring onion and salt.

2 In a large saucepan, bring enough water to the boil to submerge the chicken. Place the chicken in the pan, breast-side down. Bring the water back to the boil, then turn down the heat and simmer, covered, for 30–40 minutes. Turn the chicken over once.

3 Remove the chicken and wash in running cold water for 2 minutes to stop the cooking. Drain, then rub the oil into the skin. Set aside.

4 To prepare the rice, heat the oil in a preheated wok. Stir-fry the garlic and shallots until fragrant. Add the rice and cook for 3 minutes, stirring rapidly. Transfer to a large saucepan and add the chicken stock and salt. Bring to the boil, then turn down the heat and simmer, covered, for 20 minutes. Turn off the heat and steam for a further 5–10 minutes, or until the rice is perfectly cooked.

5 To serve, chop the chicken horizontally through the bone and skin into chunky wedges. Serve with the rice and a chilli or soy dipping sauce.

chicken steamed with rice in lotus leaves

ingredients

SERVES 4–8

450 g/1 lb glutinous rice, soaked in cold water for 2 hours

450 ml/16 fl oz cold water

1 tsp salt

1 tsp vegetable or peanut oil

4 dried lotus leaves, soaked in hot water for 1 hour

filling

100 g/3¹/₂ oz raw small prawns, shelled and deveined

2-inch/5-cm piece of very fresh root ginger

200 g/7 oz lean chicken meat, cut into bite-size strips

2 tsp light soy sauce

55 g/2 oz dried Chinese mushrooms, soaked in warm water for 20 minutes

1 tbsp vegetable or peanut oil, for frying

200 g/7 oz cha siu or pork loin

1 tbsp Shaoxing rice wine

1 tsp dark soy sauce

¹/₂ tsp white pepper

1 tsp sugar

method

1 For the filling, steam the prawns for 5 minutes and set aside. Finely grate the ginger, discarding the fibrous parts on the grater and reserving the liquid that drips through. Marinate the chicken in the light soy sauce and ginger juices for at least 20 minutes. Steam for a few minutes in the marinade. Set aside.

2 Drain the rice and place in a saucepan with the water. Bring to the boil, then add the salt and oil. Cover and cook over very low heat for 15 minutes. Divide into 8 portions and set aside.

3 Squeeze out any excess water from the mushrooms, then finely slice, discarding any tough stems. Reserve the soaking water.

4 In a preheated wok or deep saucepan, heat the oil and stir-fry the pork, prawns and mushrooms for 2 minutes. Stir in the Shaoxing, dark soy sauce, pepper and sugar. Add the reserved mushroom soaking water, if necessary.

5 Rinse and dry the lotus leaves. Place a portion of rice in the centre of each and flatten out to form a 10-cm/4-inch square. Top with the pork mixture and some pieces of chicken. Top with another portion of rice, then fold the lotus leaf to form a tight package. Steam for about 15 minutes. Let rest for 5 minutes, then serve.

chicken with vegetables & coriander rice

ingredients

SERVES 4

2 tbsp vegetable or peanut oil

1 red onion, chopped

2 garlic cloves, chopped

2.5-cm/1-inch piece root
    ginger, peeled and
    chopped

2 skinless, boneless chicken
    breasts, cut into strips

115 g/4 oz white mushrooms

400 g/14 oz canned
    coconut milk

55 g/2 oz sugar snap peas,
    trimmed and halved
    lengthways

2 tbsp soy sauce

1 tbsp fish sauce

rice

1 tbsp vegetable or peanut oil

1 red onion, sliced

350 g/12 oz rice, cooked and
    cooled

225 g/8 oz pak choi, torn into
    large pieces

handful of fresh coriander,
    chopped

2 tbsp Thai soy sauce

method

1 Heat the oil in a wok or large frying pan and
sauté the onion, garlic and ginger together for
1–2 minutes.

2 Add the chicken and mushrooms and cook
over high heat until browned. Add the coconut
milk, sugar snap peas and sauces and bring
to the boil. Simmer gently for 4–5 minutes
until tender.

3 Heat the oil for the rice in a separate wok or
large frying pan and cook the onion until
softened, but not browned. Add the cooked
rice, pak choi and fresh coriander and heat
gently until the leaves have wilted and the rice
is hot. Sprinkle over the soy sauce and serve
immediately with the chicken.

chicken biryani

ingredients

SERVES 8

1 1/2 tsp finely chopped fresh
    root ginger
1 1/2 tsp crushed fresh garlic
1 tbsp garam masala
1 tsp chilli powder
1/2 tsp ground turmeric
2 tsp salt
5 green/white cardamom
    pods, crushed
300 ml/10 fl oz plain yogurt
1.5 kg/3 lb 5 oz chicken,
    skinned and cut into
    8 pieces
150 ml/5 fl oz milk
1 tsp saffron strands
6 tbsp ghee
2 onions, sliced
450 g/1 lb basmati rice
2 cinnamon sticks
4 black peppercorns
1 tsp black cumin seeds
4 fresh green chillies
4 tbsp lemon juice
2–3 tbsp finely chopped fresh
    coriander leaves

method

1 Blend the ginger, garlic, garam masala, chilli powder, turmeric, half the salt and the cardamoms together in a bowl. Add the yogurt and chicken pieces and mix well. Cover and marinate in the refrigerator for 3 hours.

2 Boil the milk in a small saucepan, pour over the saffron and set aside.

3 Heat the ghee in a large saucepan. Add the onions and cook until golden. Transfer half of the onions and ghee to a bowl and set aside.

4 Place the rice, cinnamon sticks, peppercorns and black cumin seeds in a saucepan of water. Bring to the boil and remove from the heat when the rice is half-cooked. Drain and place in a bowl. Mix with the remaining salt.

5 Chop the chillies and set aside. Add the chicken mixture to the pan containing the onions. Add half each of the chopped green chillies, lemon juice, coriander and saffron milk. Add the rice, then the rest of the ingredients, including the reserved onions and ghee. Cover tightly and cook over low heat for 1 hour. Check that the meat is cooked through; if it is not cooked, return to the heat, and cook for a further 15 minutes. Mix well before serving.